Knit Two

Knit Two

ANGELA KING

This edition published 1984 by
Book Club Associates
by arrangement with
William Collins plc
First published in Great Britain 1984
© Knitting patterns Angela King 1984
© William Collins plc 1984

Jacket photograph by Colin Thomas

Filmset in Souvenir by Cheney & Sons Ltd, Banbury

Printed in Great Britain by William Collins plc, Glasgow

ACKNOWLEDGEMENTS

Once again, warmest thanks to all my wonderful knitters, for all the hard work and cups of tea and coffee.

May Begg
Irene Bonstein
Janet Borg
Angela Chapman
Jenny Davis
Nora Giorgi
Mandy Goldman
Sally King
Christine Lovegrove
Mary McDowell
Mrs Noble

Miss E. Patrick
Fusako Ridley
Sue Rose
Betty Truman
Marjorie Vennall

and thanks also to:

Barbara Britton
Jean Dyott
Rosalinde Goalen
Dianne Howes

The author and publishers gratefully acknowledge the help of the following magazines, wool companies and photographers who have given permission for their photographs to be reproduced in this book. Photographs were supplied courtesy of:

Company (*Just Checking* – photograph: Tony McGee; *Reds*; *Valentine* – photograph: Richard Lohr)
Cosmopolitan (*Déjà Vu* – photograph: Neil Kirk; *Tangled Up In Blue* – photograph: Toscani; *Carte Blanche* – photograph: Toscani; *Bel-Ami* – photograph: Perry Ogden)
Family Circle (*Saddle Tramp*; *Gilda*)
Honey (*Bodyline Tactics* – photograph: Martin Brading; *Fast and Loose* – photograph: Martin Brading; *Side Kick* – photograph: Monty Coles; *Street Legal* – photograph: Martin Brading)
Living (*Spare Rib*)
Pingouin (photographs: Tony Boase – *Sunny* [leaflet no. 8355]; *Flashback* [leaflet no. 8354]; *Country Girls* [leaflet no. 8353])
She (*Think Pink*)
Sunday (supplement to *The News of the World*) (*Hussy* – photograph: Jane England; *Flirt* – photograph: Jane England)
TV Times Creative Look Book (*Subtle Hint* – photograph: Paul Fletcher)
Vogue Pattern Book (*Easy Rider* – photograph: Tony Boase)
Weekend (*Appeal Against The Light* – photograph: Tommy Candler; *Hit On The Leg Side* – photograph: Tommy Candler)
Woman (*Broadway Baby*; *Road Runner*)
Woman's Realm (*Angel Delight*)
Woman's Weekly (*Manor Born*)

Thanks also to the following for providing clothes and
accessories in these photographs:
Sea Cruise (trousers by Ralph Lauren at Polo; hat by
Bodymap; shoes from Rider)
Lace (skirt by Jacqueline Hancher; tights by Chantal
Thomas for Wolsey; shoes from Rider)
Tricot Treat (jodhpurs by Culture Shock at Etcetera; belt
from Laurence Corner)
One Armed Bandit (skirt by Bodymap)
Beau Jest (skirt and gloves from Browns, beret by Kangol,
shoes from Rider)
Mosaic (trousers from Miss Selfridge)
Photographs: Tony McGee; hair by Joel O'Sullivan at
Burlingtons

FOR ADVICE ABOUT YARN

**Pingouin
(French Wools Ltd),**
7-11 Lexington Street,
London, W1R 4BU
Tel: 01-439 8891

Patons and Baldwin Ltd,
Alloa, Clackmannanshire,
Scotland, FK10 1EG
Tel: Alloa (0259) 723431

Sirdar Ltd,
PO Box 31,
Alverthorpe, Wakefield,
West Yorkshire
Tel: Wakefield (0924) 371501

H. G. Twilley Ltd,
Roman Mills, Stamford,
Lincolnshire, PE9 1BG
Tel: Stamford (0780) 52661

Maxwell Cartlidge Ltd,
PO Box 33,
Colchester, Essex, CO1 1EQ
Tel: Colchester (0206) 41275

Hayfield Textiles Ltd,
Hayfield Mills,
Glusburn, Keighley,
West Yorkshire, BD20 8QP
Tel: Cross Hills (0535) 33333

Ries Wools Ltd,
242-243 High Holborn,
London, WC1
Tel: 01-242 7721 (for advice on
Pingouin, Patons, Sirdar, Twilleys and
Hayfield yarns)

Contents

Introduction

You may feel that your knitting skills are minimal, but even if you can do only plain knitting, purl and cables, you can make yourself a stunning summer and winter wardrobe. Aim for big knits in simple shapes, using huge needles or the yarn knitted double, or knit a basic square with loads of chunky texture or a bold cable pattern. Thick textured yarns hide beginners' mistakes and, in any case, shouldn't be knitted up too neatly – inexperienced knitters have an advantage here, because rough uneven stitches are part of the look.

If you can fair isle, try something in big bold checks, or test your manual dexterity with a witty trompe l'oeil design. They look most impressive when finished, but yards of plain knitting make up for the intense concentration needed when working from the chart. (If you can't knit fair isle, but long to try, begin by knitting a sample square using thick yarn in two colours, and practise reading from a chart.)

For summer, you could make something cropped and knitted from side to side – whether tight to the body or wide is up to you – in cool crunchy cotton, or using an exciting new yarn like rags or raffia. Have fun with stripes: melting them together by using pastel shades, or knitting them in stark bands of black, cream and beige.

Cost-conscious knitters pick beautiful classics, which last forever and justify the price of specialist yarns such as silk. These must be knitted neatly, with particular attention paid to the sewing up, but many are now designed with novice knitters in mind.

Certain techniques in knitting do take a long time to master, but if you love colour and texture, there is no end to the beautiful things you can make, even in plain knitting.

Some Useful Advice

Fair isle (knitting with colours) is one of the most exciting and enjoyable of all knitting techniques. The creative possibilities are absolutely endless, but you do need *patience* – and lots of it, especially at the beginning.

The main problem with fair isle is what to do with the colours at the back of the work. If you know what you are doing, the back of your knitting will be as neat as the front. If you are not doing it properly, a terrible snarl of different colours will bunch at the back, and the front will be full of gaping holes.

Some fair isle patterns are in word form but most are worked from a chart, so study this first.

Reading a chart
Each *symbol* in the chart represents a colour. To find out which colour, look at the *key*. Each square of the chart refers to one stitch and one row. The chart gives you one *repeat* of the pattern. The number of stitches in the repeat should divide into the number of stitches in your row, although there may be a *selvedge stitch* at each end of every row. (Selvedge stitches are those stitches at each end of every row that you use for sewing up.)

The numbers printed at the sides of the chart are the *rows* which make up the pattern repeat.

Fair isle is nearly always worked in *stocking stitch*. Therefore all *odd-numbered* rows on the chart are *knit* rows and are worked from *right to left* on the chart. All *even-numbered* rows are *purl* rows, and worked from *left to right* on the chart.

Dealing with the yarn at the back
In fair isle, one or more colours have to be carried along the row while not in use. This can be done by either weaving or stranding.

Weaving The yarn not in use is carried over the yarn in use for one stitch, then

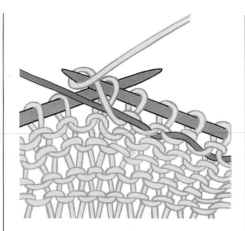

Weaving

under it for the next stitch on the wrong side of the work. This can make the fabric rather stiff and solid so the method is best for socks and gloves.

Stranding If the different colours are spaced only four or five stitches apart, strand the yarn not in use by carrying it across the back of the work. *Twist* the yarns concerned when changing colours to avoid holes.

If the different colours are spaced very widely apart, you can still use the stranding method, but this time catch the colour not in use by dropping it over the colour in use at every four or five stitches.

When very large areas of one colour are part of a design, it is best not to strand or weave, but to use different balls of yarn for each area, remembering to *twist* to avoid holes.

When either weaving or stranding, remember to do both *loosely* or you will

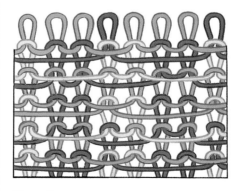

Stranding

achieve an appalling concertina effect. To avoid this, gently spread out the last eight or ten stitches you have just worked along the right hand needle, so that the work is slightly stretched. Now take up the next colour and continue knitting.

Try to keep the back of the work as tidy as you can. For an even finish, one colour should always be kept above and the other beneath.

Twisting

Knitting in the ends
The bit of extra trouble it takes to do this as you go along will save you hours of boring darning in at the sewing up stage. When you have finished with a colour, knit in this yarn by dropping it over the yarn in use. Knit a stitch and repeat three or four times before cutting the end.

Dealing with tangles
Try not to let the yarns get too badly tangled at the back – sort them out before they become a bundle of knots.

The ways you can keep the yarns separate are:

1. Keep the colours in small balls and loop a slip knot or elastic band over each to prevent them unwinding.
2. Keep each ball in a jam jar on the floor.
3. Use special bobbins.

Finally, when attempting your first fair isle, do knit a stitch sample. You will save yourself so much time and effort if you check your tension first and practise the pattern repeats before you start the garment. You may be glowing with pride when you have finally managed to complete the pieces, but don't wreck the whole thing by dreadful sewing up. Sew up the pieces with the *right side* facing you, matching up the pattern as you go.

Knitting with a circular needle

Modern sweaters sometimes have a 'funnel' collar, which is best worked on a circular needle so that there is no seam. Many people are put off as soon as circular needles are mentioned although they are, in fact, very easy to use.

They are made of flexible plastic with a knitting needle at each end, and can be bought in various lengths. If you buy one that is too long it will stretch the work out of shape, so aim to buy one which will enable the stitches to reach the needle points at each end without stretching the knitting beyond the correct tension. It is also quite all right to use a needle which is shorter than this — as long as the stitches are not uncomfortably crowded.

Circular needle

Knitting with silk

Knitting with silk is more expensive than with wool, but the rich, glowing colours and sensuous feel of the finished garment are more than worth the extra money. (One consolation is that, although the price is roughly three times that of a ball of wool, a ball of silk has greater yardage so it will go much further.)

Like cotton, silk is inelastic, so you must knit *firmly*. If you are using a wool pattern for your silk, remember that silk does not stretch at all. Loosely worked rib will *drop*, so use smaller sized needles than you would for wool.

Knitting with silk is a seductive experience in itself and, unlike wool, it feels wonderful against the skin.

Washing
Silk is easy to care for and should be hand-washed, avoiding harsh detergents. Use tepid or warm water and do not rub or wring. The use of a fabric conditioner is recommended. Dry the garment by rolling it in a towel first before laying it out flat to dry thoroughly. Press it lightly while it is still slightly damp, if necessary. A gentle shake will remove any slight stiffness caused by drying.

How to knit

Casting on: two needle method

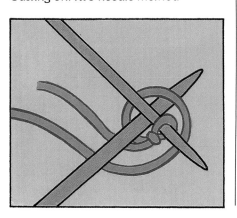

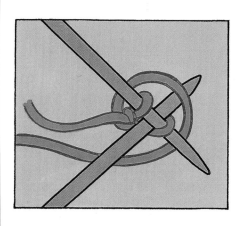

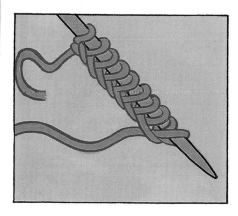

Casting on

The two needle method Make a slip loop in the yarn, leaving a short length for sewing up. Place the loop onto the left hand needle. Firmly grasp the short length in the left hand, then insert the point of the right hand needle behind the loop on the left hand needle. Wind the yarn round the right hand needle and draw through. Pass the new loop onto the left hand needle and tighten.

Insert the right hand needle between the two loops on the left hand needle, wind yarn round right hand needle and draw through. Pass the new loop onto the left hand needle as before.

Continue in this way until you have cast on the required number of stitches.

How to knit a stitch

Hold the needle with the cast on stitches in the left hand. With the yarn at the back of the work, insert the right hand needle into the front of the first loop on the left hand needle, front to back, left to right. Wind the yarn round the point of the right hand needle and draw a loop through the loop on the left hand needle, while slipping this left hand stitch. The new stitch is now on the right hand needle.

How to knit a stitch

How to purl a stitch

Hold the needle with the cast on stitches in the left hand. With the yarn at the front of the work, insert the right hand needle into the front of the first stitch, back to front, right to left. Take the yarn round the point of the right hand needle over the top and under, from right to left. Draw this loop through the stitch on the left hand needle, while slipping the left hand stitch. The new stitch is now on the right hand needle.

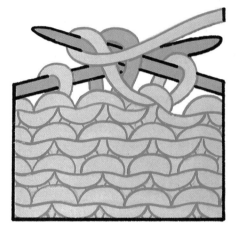

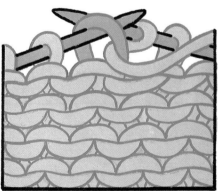

How to purl a stitch

Some simple stitches

Garter stitch Knit every stitch of every row.

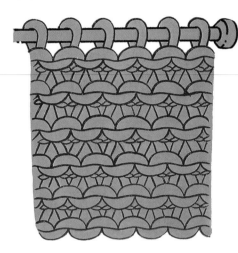

Garter stitch

Stocking stitch Knit the first row and purl the second row, repeating these two rows. The knit side is the right side.

Stocking stitch

Reversed stocking stitch Purl the first row and knit the second row, repeating these two rows. The purl side is the right side.

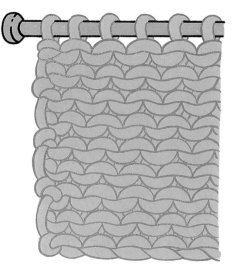

Reversed stocking stitch

Moss stitch Knit the first stitch and purl the second stitch, to the end of the row. On the second row, purl all the stitches that face you as knit, and knit all the stitches that face you as purl, repeating these two rows.

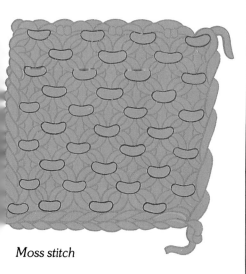

Moss stitch

Ribbing Usually single or double ribbing, although there are others. Single ribbing is worked by alternating knit and purl stitches to the end of a row. On the second row, you knit all the knit stitches and purl all the purl stitches. For double ribbing, alternate two knit and two purl stitches along the row, working stitches as they face you on the second row.

Tension

If you are following someone else's pattern, you *must* knit to tension. Tension means how tightly or loosely the knitting is worked. If you hate knitting a tension square, do a careful check on your actual work and measure the number of stitches and rows to the number of centimetres quoted at the top of the pattern. If you have fewer stitches than the given tension, change your needles to a size *smaller*. If you have more stitches, change your needle to a size *larger*. If you neglect this check, your garment will probably come out the wrong size.

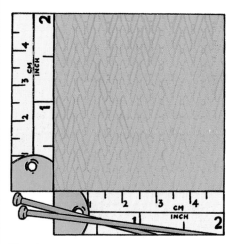

Tension

Abbreviations

It is vital to read the abbreviations at the beginning of any pattern. These are not standardised and one designer may use the same abbreviation as another while meaning something completely different. So check them before you begin to knit – *never* assume you know what they all mean.

Joining in yarn

To avoid holes, always join in yarn at the end of a row – the long ends will be useful for sewing up afterwards.

Measurements

Like tension, measurements must be checked carefully so that the garment comes out the size that the designer intended.

Casting off

Knit the first two stitches of the row. With the point of the left hand needle, lift the stitch furthest to the right on the right hand needle over the stitch next to it, leaving one stitch on the right hand needle. Knit one more stitch, making two stitches on the right hand needle. Lift the one furthest to the right over the second, as before. Continue in this way until only one stitch remains. Cut the yarn and pass it through the stitch, pulling tightly to fasten off.

Casting off

Déjà Vu

Trompe l'oeil (trick the eye) tunic with belt and beads. The illusion of a wide leather belt and necklace is created by fair isling them as part of the tunic, which buttons at the back.

MATERIALS

9 (10, 10) 50 g. balls Pingouin Confort in main shade (black) and 1 (1, 1) ball in each of 4 contrast shades (fuchsia, grey, white and pink); a pair each 3¼ mm. (no. 10) and 3¾ mm. (no. 9) knitting needles; a stitch-holder; a medium-size crochet hook; one small black button.

TENSION

24 stitches and 30 rows to 10 cm. over stocking stitch, using 3¾ mm. needles.

MEASUREMENTS

To fit bust 34 (36, 38) in., 86 (91, 97) cm.
Length 30½ (31, 31½) in., 77 (79, 80) cm.
Sleeve seam (all sizes) 17 in., 43 cm.

ABBREVIATIONS

k., knit; p., purl; st(s)., stitch(es); alt., alternate; beg., beginning; cont., continue; dec., decrease; foll., following; inc(s)., increase(s); rem., remain(ing); sep., separately; st. st., stocking stitch; tog., together; MS, main shade (black); A, first contrast shade (fuchsia); B, second contrast (grey); C, third contrast (white); D, fourth contrast (pink).

NOTE

See page 10 for information on reading a chart.

INSTRUCTIONS

Back

With 3¼ mm. needles and MS, cast on 114 (120, 126) sts. Work in k. 1, p. 1 rib for 4 cm.
Change to 3¾ mm. needles and work 72 rows in st. st. (see page 12) **.
Change to A and work 38 rows in st. st.
Change to MS and work 52 rows in st. st.

To shape armhole Cast off 7 sts. at beg. of next 2 rows and 3 sts. at beg. of foll. 2 rows. Dec. 1 st. at each end of every alt. row until 88 (94, 100) sts. rem. Cont. straight in st. st. until work measures 14 (15, 16) cm. from beg. of armhole shaping, ending with a p. row.

To work back neck opening K. 44 (47, 50), turn, leaving rem. sts. on a spare needle. Work 1 row. Work 8 rows fair isle from Chart 1 (right back neck), thus ending with a p. row.

To shape neck Next row: Keeping fair isle correct, k. 33 (36, 39), k. 2 tog., slip rem. 9 sts. onto a stitch-holder for Neckband. Cont. to work fair isle as on Chart but dec. 1 st. at neck edge on foll. 3 alt. rows. Cast off rem. 31 (34, 37) sts. With right side facing, rejoin MS to rem. sts. and work 2 rows in st. st. Work 8 rows fair isle from Chart 1 (left back neck), thus ending with a p. row.

To shape neck Next row: Slip first 9 sts. onto a stitch-holder for Neckband, rejoin yarn to rem. sts. and k. 2 tog., k. to end, keeping fair isle correct. Cont. as on Chart, but dec. 1 st. at neck edge on foll. 3 rows. Cast off rem. 31 (34, 37) sts.

Front

Work as for Back to **. Work 38 rows fair isle from Chart 2. Change to MS and work 36 (40, 44) rows in st. st. Work 16 (12, 8) rows fair isle from Chart 3.

To shape armholes Work as for Back armhole shaping, at the same time cont. in fair isle from Chart 3 until row 50 has been worked.

To shape neck K. 36 (39, 42), turn. Complete each side sep. Dec. 1 st. at neck edge on every alt. row until 31 (34, 37) sts. rem. When row 72 of Chart 3 has been completed, cast off. Leave centre 16 sts. on a spare needle; rejoin yarn to rem. sts. at neck edge and work other side to match, reversing shapings.

Sleeves

With 3¼ mm. needles and MS, cast on 52 (56, 60) sts. Work in k. 1, p. 1 rib for 7 cm., working 18 incs. evenly spaced along last rib row – 70 (74, 78) sts.
Change to 3¾ mm. needles and work in st. st., inc. 1 st. at each end of every foll. tenth row until there are 82 (86, 90) sts. Work straight until sleeve measures 43 cm. from beg., ending with a p. row.

To shape armholes Cast off 7 sts. at beg. of next 2 rows, then dec. 1 st. at

Chart 1

Note: Chart is worked in 2 parts of 44 (47, 50) sts. each.

KEY
Pingouin Confort
☐ MS (black)
✕ C (white)
● D (pink)

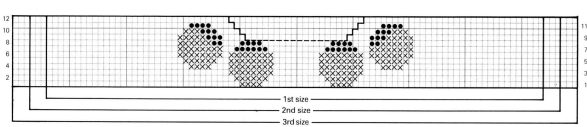

LEFT BACK NECK   RIGHT BACK NECK

Déjà Vu

Chart 2

KEY
Pingouin Confort

□ MS (black) ✕ A (fuchsia) ● B (grey)

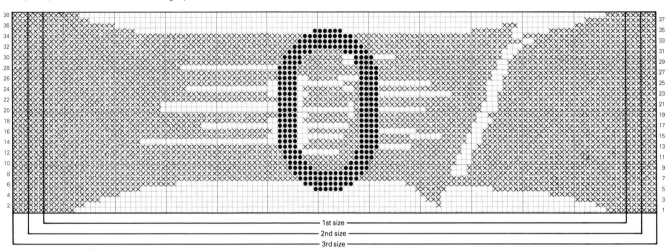

1st size
2nd size
3rd size

Chart 3

KEY
Pingouin Confort

□ MS (black) ✕ C (white) ● D (pink)

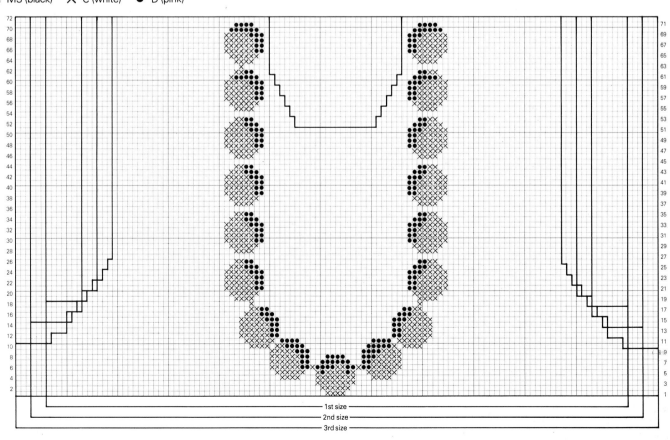

1st size
2nd size
3rd size

Déjà Vu

each end of every alt. row until 26 sts. rem. Cast off 5 sts. at beg. of next 2 rows. Cast off rem. sts.

Neckband

Join shoulder seams. With 3¼ mm. needles and right side facing and with MS, beg. at left side of back neck opening, k. 9 sts. across left back neck, pick up and k. 21 sts. up left back neck and down left front neck, k. 16 sts. across front neck, then pick up and k. 21 sts. up right front neck and down right back neck, k. 9 sts. across right back neck – 76 sts.

Work in k. 1, p. 1 rib for 7 rows. Cast off ribwise.

TO MAKE UP

Set in sleeves. Join sleeve seams and side seams, matching belt pattern. Work a row of double crochet along back neck opening.

Crochet a loop on left hand edge of back neck opening. Sew on button.

Think Pink

MATERIALS

11 (12) 50 g. balls Pingouin Coton Naturel 8 Fils in pale pink; a pair each 3¼ mm. (no. 10) and 4 mm. (no. 8) knitting needles (long length); a cable needle.

TENSION

Approximately 21 stitches and 31 rows to 10 cm. over stocking stitch, using 4 mm. needles.

MEASUREMENTS

To fit bust 32-34 (36-38) in., 81-86 (91-97) cm. loosely.
Length (both sizes) 15½ in., 39 cm.
Sleeve (both sizes) 16½ in., 42 cm. measured when straight and with cuff not turned back.

ABBREVIATIONS

k., knit; p., purl; st(s)., stitch(es); alt., alternate; beg., begin(ning); cont., continue; C3B, slip next st. onto cable needle and hold at back of work, k. 2, then p. 1 from cable needle; C3F, slip next 2 sts. onto cable needle and hold at front of work, p. 1, then k. 2 from cable needle; dec(s)., decrease(s); foll., following; inc., increase(e)(ing); MB, make bobble by working (k. 1, p. 1, k. 1, p. 1, k. 1, p. 1) all into next st., then lift 2nd, 3rd, 4th, 5th and 6th sts. over the 1st st.; patt., pattern; rem., remain(ing); rep., repeat; st. st., stocking stitch.

NOTE

The garment is worked in one piece.

INSTRUCTIONS

Beg. at lower edge of front. With 3¼ mm. needles, cast on 102 (110) sts. Work in k. 1, p. 1 rib for 4 cm., ending with a wrong side row.
Next row: Rib 48 (52), rib twice into next

(see page 12)

Cropped wide cotton sweater in palest pink is knitted all in one piece and has an Aran diamond and bobble pattern up the front and back. The neck is allowed to roll over.

5 sts., rib 48 (52) – 107 (115) sts.
Change to 4 mm. needles and work in the foll. patt.:
Row 1 (wrong side): P. 46 (50), k. 5, p. 5, k. 5, p. 46 (50).
Row 2: K. 46 (50), p. 5, k. 2, MB, k. 2, p. 5, k. 46 (50).
Row 3: As row 1.
Row 4: K. 46 (50), p. 5, MB, k. 3, MB, p. 5, k. 46 (50).
Row 5: As row 1.
Row 6: As row 2.
Row 7: As row 1.
Row 8: K. 46 (50), p. 4, C3B, p. 1, C3F, p. 4, k. 46 (50).
Row 9: P. 46 (50), k. 4, p. 2, k. 1, p. 1, k. 1, p. 2, k. 4, p. 46 (50).
Row 10: K. 46 (50), p. 3, C3B, k. 1, p. 1, k. 1, C3F, p. 3, k. 46 (50).
Row 11: P. 46 (50), k. 3, p. 3, k. 1, p. 1, k. 1, p. 3, k. 3, p. 46 (50).
Row 12: K. 46 (50), p. 2, C3B, (p. 1, k. 1) twice, p. 1, C3F, p. 2, k. 46 (50).
Row 13: P. 46 (50), k. 2, p. 2, (k. 1, p. 1) three times, k. 1, p. 2, k. 2, p. 46 (50).
Row 14: K. 46 (50), p. 1, C3B, (k. 1, p. 1) three times, k. 1, C3F, p. 1, k. 46 (50).
Row 15: P. 46 (50), k. 1, p. 3, (k. 1, p. 1) four times, p. 2, k. 1, p. 46 (50).
Row 16: K. 46 (50), p. 1, k. 2, (p. 1, k. 1) four times, p. 1, k. 2, p. 1, k. 46 (50).
Row 17: As row 15.
Row 18: K. 46 (50), p. 1, C3F, (k. 1, p. 1) three times, k. 1, C3B, p. 1, k. 46 (50).
Row 19: As row 13.
Row 20: K. 46 (50), p. 2, C3F, (p. 1, k. 1) twice, p. 1, C3B, p. 2, k. 46 (50).
Row 21: As row 11.
Row 22: K. 46 (50), p. 3, C3F, k. 1, p. 1, k. 1, C3B, p. 3, k. 46 (50).
Row 23: As row 9.
Row 24: K. 46 (50), p. 4, C3F, p. 1, C3B, p. 4, k. 46 (50).
These 24 rows form patt. Rep. rows 1 to 7 once more.

To shape for sleeves Keeping continuity of patt. in centre, inc. 1 st. at each end of next 10 rows, thus ending on a row 17 of patt. – 127 (135) sts.
Now cast on 22 sts. at beg. of next 8 rows – 303 (311) sts.
Cont. straight with centre patt. panel and rem. sts. in st. st. (see page 12) until the fourth complete patt. has been worked, ending with a right side row.
Next row: P. to end, but work 5 decs. over centre panel. Cont. in st. st. for 6 (8) rows, ending with a p. row.

To shape neck *Next row:* K. 126 (130), cast off next 46 sts., k. to end.
Next row: P. 126 (130), cast on 46 sts., p. to end.
Cont. for Back, working 7 (9) rows in st. st., inc. 5 sts. over centre 5 sts. on last row – 303 (311) sts.
Now work the Aran patt. over the 15 centre sts. as before, but beg. at row 7 and working to row 24, then rep. rows 1 to 24 again. Work rows 1 to 5 of next patt.

To shape for sleeves Keeping continuity of centre panel, cast off 22 sts. at beg. of next 8 rows, then dec. 1 st. at each end of next 10 rows – 107 (115) sts.
Cont. straight until the fourth patt. has been completed, then work rows 1 to 6 once more, working 5 decs. at centre of last row – 102 (110) sts.
Change to 3¼ mm. needles and work in rib to match front. Cast off ribwise.

TO MAKE UP

Join side and sleeve seams, sewing 19 cm. of seam at lower part of sleeve to allow for cuff turning back. The neck border will roll back on itself.

Hit On The Leg Side

MATERIALS

18 50 g. balls Pingouin Coton Naturel 8 Fils in main shade and 1 ball in each of 2 contrast shades; a pair each 3¼ mm. (no. 10) and 4 mm. (no. 8) knitting needles; a cable needle; two shoulder pads (optional).

TENSION

20 stitches and 26 rows to 10 cm. over stocking stitch, using 4 mm. needles.

MEASUREMENTS

To fit one size only.
Bust 34-38 in., 86-96 cm.
Length 34 in., 86 cm. (adjustable).
Sleeve seam 9 in., 23 cm.

ABBREVIATIONS

k., knit; p., purl; st(s)., stitch(es); alt., alternate; beg., beginning; cont., continue; C10F, slip next 5 sts. onto cable needle and place at back of work, k. 5, then k. 5 from cable needle; dec., decreas(e)(ing); foll., following; inc., increase; patt. pattern; rem., remain-(ing); rep., repeat; sep., separately; tog., together; MS, main shade; CS1, first contrast shade; CS2, second contrast shade.

INSTRUCTIONS

Back

** With 3¼ mm. needles and MS, cast on 118 sts. Work in k. 1, p. 1 rib for 8 rows.

Classic cricket sweater dress has striped bands and bold cables, separated by strips of stocking stitch.

Change to CS1 and work in k. 1, p. 1 rib for 2 rows.
Break CS1 and with MS, work in k. 1, p. 1 rib for 4 rows.
Change to CS2 and work in k. 1, p. 1 rib for 2 rows.
Break CS2 and with MS, work in k. 1, p. 1 rib for 5 rows.
Inc. row: Rib 12, * inc. in next st., rib 3; rep. from * twenty-three times more, rib 10 – 142 sts.
Change to 4 mm. needles and work the foll. patt. in MS:
Row 1: K. 2, * p. 4, k. 10, p. 4, k. 2 *; rep. from * to * to end.
Row 2: P. 2, * k. 4, p. 10, k. 4, p. 2 *; rep. from * to * to end.
Rows 3 to 6: Rep. rows 1 and 2 twice more.
Row 7: K. 2, * p. 4, C10F, p. 4, k. 2 *; rep. from * to * to end.
Row 8: As row 2.
Rows 9 to 14: Rep. rows 1 and 2 three times more.
These 14 rows form patt. When patt. has been completed ten times in all, work rows 1 to 8 once more. (Length can be adjusted here if desired)**.

To shape armholes Keeping patt. correct, cast off 6 sts. at beg. of next 2 rows, 4 sts. at beg. of foll. 2 rows, then dec. 1 st. at each end of every alt. row five times in all – 112 sts.

Cont. straight until work measures 19 cm. from beg. of armhole shaping.

To shape neck Work 36, cast off centre 40 sts., work to end. Finish each side sep. Dec. 1 st. at neck edge on every row until 30 sts. rem. Cast off, but dec. 5 sts. over cable as you do so to make a tight edge. Rejoin yarn and complete other side of neck to match.

Front

Work as for Back from ** to **.

To shape armholes and neck *Next row:* Cast off 6 sts., patt. until there are 64 sts. on right hand needle, slip next 2 sts. onto a safety-pin, patt. to end of row. Work each side of neck sep.
Next row: Cast off 6 sts., patt. to end.
Next row: Work 2 tog., patt. to end.
Next row: Cast off 4 sts., patt. to end.
*** Dec. 1 st. at each end of next and foll. 4 alt. rows – 49 sts.
Now keep armhole edge straight but cont. to dec. on alt. rows at neck edge until 30 sts. rem.
Work straight until armhole matches Back. Cast off, dec. over cable as for Back.
*** With wrong side facing, join yarn to neck edge of rem. sts. and patt. to end of row.
Next row: Cast off 4 sts., patt. to last 2 sts., work 2 tog.
Work 1 row without shaping, then work as for first side from *** to ***.

Sleeves

With 3¼ mm. needles and MS, cast on 72 sts. Work 21 rows in rib with stripes exactly as for Back.
Inc. row: * Rib 3, inc. in next st.; rep. from * to end – 90 sts.

Change to 4 mm. needles and work cable patt. as follows:

Row 1: P. 4, k. 2, * p. 4, k. 10, p. 4, k. 2; rep. from * to last 4 sts., p. 4.

Row 2: K. 4, p. 2, * k. 4, p. 10, k. 4, p. 2; rep. from * to last 4 sts., k. 4.

Cont. to work cable as set for Back until work measures 23 cm. from beg., ending with a wrong side row.

To shape armholes Cast off 6 sts. at beg. of next 2 rows, and 4 sts. at beg. of foll. 2 rows. Dec. 1 st. at each end of every alt. row until 40 sts. rem. Cast off 6 sts. at beg. of next 2 rows. Cast off rem. sts. but dec. over cables as for Back. Join left shoulder seam.

Neckband

With 3¼ mm. needles and right side facing and with MS, pick up and k. 42 sts. along back neck, 44 sts. along left neck edge, work across the 2 sts. of centre neck and pick up and k. 44 sts. along right neck edge.

Work 3 rows in k. 1, p. 1 rib but dec. 1 st. at either side of centre 2 sts. on every alt. row.

Change to CS1 and work 2 rows in k. 1, p. 1 rib.

Break CS1 and work 4 rows in MS, then work 2 rows in CS2.

Work 2 further rows in MS, then cast off ribwise.

TO MAKE UP

Join right shoulder seam and neckband. Set in sleeves. Join sleeve seams and side seams. Sew in shoulder pads if required.

Sea Cruise

MATERIALS

Knitted in Maxwell Cartlidge 'Silks' (100 per cent pure silk) available by mail order only from Maxwell Cartlidge, PO Box 33, Colchester, Essex, CO1 1EQ.
7 (8, 8) 50 g. balls Maxwell Cartlidge Silk in sky (shade S5E); a pair each 3 mm. (no. 11) and 3¼ mm. (no. 10) knitting needles; a circular 3 mm. (no. 11) needle; a stitch-holder.

TENSION

34 stitches and 36 rows to 10 cm. over flat rib, using 3¼ mm. needles.

MEASUREMENTS

To fit bust 34 (36, 38) in., 86 (91, 97) cm.
Length 21¾ (22½, 23¼) in., 55 (57, 59) cm.
Sleeve (all sizes) 16½ in., 43 cm.

ABBREVIATIONS

k., knit; p., purl; st(s)., stitch(es); alt., alternate; beg., beginning; cont., continue; dec(s)., decrease(s); foll., following; inc(s)., increase(s); patt., pattern; rem., remain(ing); rep., repeat.

NOTE

See page 11 for information on knitting with silk.

INSTRUCTIONS

Back

With 3 mm. needles, cast on 151 (161, 171) sts. Work in k. 1, p. 1 rib for 6 cm., working 11 incs. evenly along last rib row – 162 (172, 182) sts.
Change to 3¼ mm. needles and work the foll. patt.:
Row 1: * P. 2, k. 8; rep. from * to last 2 sts., p. 2.
Row 2: K. the k. sts. and p. the p. sts. as they face you.

Pure silk pale blue sweater in flat rib with padded shoulders and a square neckline.
Easy

These 2 rows form patt. Cont. in patt. until work measures 36 (37, 38) cm. from beg.

To shape armholes Cast off 8 sts. at beg. of next 2 rows and 3 sts. at beg. of foll. 2 rows. Dec 1 st. at each end of every foll. alt. row until 122 (132, 142) sts. rem. **.
Cont. straight until work measures 17 (18, 19) cm. from beg. of armhole shaping.

To shape neck Work 38 (43, 48), turn: work on these sts. only. Dec. 1 st. at neck edge on next 6 rows. Work 1 row, then cast off. Slip the middle 46 sts. onto a stitch-holder to be worked later as Neckband. Rejoin yarn and complete other side of neck to match.

Front

Exactly as Back to **. Work straight until work measures 7 (8, 9) cm. from beg. of armhole shaping.

To shape square neck Work 32 (37, 42), turn: work on these sts. only. When length to shoulder matches Back, cast off. Slip the centre 58 sts. onto a spare needle to be worked later as square neckband. Rejoin yarn and complete other side of neck to match.

Sleeves

With 3 mm. needles, cast on 61 (69, 77) sts. Work in k. 1, p. 1 rib for 7 cm., working 31 (33, 35) incs. evenly along last rib row – 92 (102, 112) sts.
Change to 3¼ mm. needles and work in flat rib as set for Back but inc. 1 st. at each end of every foll. tenth row until there are 112 (122, 132) sts. Cont. straight until work measures 43 cm. from beg.

To shape armholes Cast off 8 sts. at beg. of next 2 rows and 3 sts. at beg. of

foll. 2 rows. Dec. 1 st. at each end of every alt. row until 50 sts. rem.
Cast off 10 sts. at beg. of next 2 rows, then cast off rem. sts.

Neckband

Join shoulder seams. With circular 3 mm. needle and right side facing, work across the 46 sts. of back neck in k. 1, p. 1 rib, beg. p. and dec. 1 st. at centre, then pick up and k. 10 sts. along back left neck, 38 sts. along front left neck, 1 st. at left corner (marking this st. with a safety-pin), then beg. p. work in rib over the 58 sts. of front neck, working 5 decs. over these sts., pick up 1 st. at right corner (marking this st. with a safety-pin), 38 sts. along right front neck and 10 sts. along right back neck – 196 sts.
Now work in rounds of k. 1, p. 1 rib, but dec. 1 st. at each side of the sts. marked with a pin (which are worked k. on the right side and p. on the wrong side) on every alt. round. When 8 rounds have been completed, cast off ribwise.

TO MAKE UP

Press all pieces of garment except rib on the reverse side with a warm iron and a damp cloth. Set in sleeves. Join sleeve seams and side seams. Press all seams.

Sandpiper

MATERIALS

4 (5) 50 g. balls Patons Cotton Top in main shade – khaki (shade 6412), 1 (2) balls in each of 3 contrast shades – blue (6436), lilac (6440) and green (6416) and 2 (2) balls in each of 2 further contrast shades – yellow (6420) and rose (6424); a pair each 4 mm. (no. 8) and 3¾ mm. (no. 9) knitting needles; a darning needle.

TENSION

20 stitches and 29 rows to 10 cm.

MEASUREMENTS

To fit bust 32-34 (36-38) in., 81-86 (91-97) cm.
Length (both sizes) 19 in., 48 cm.
Sleeve (both sizes) 15 in., 37 cm.

ABBREVIATIONS

k., knit; p., purl; st(s)., stitch(es); dec., decrease; foll., following; g-st., garter stitch; inc., increase; patt., pattern; rem., remain(ing); st. st., stocking stitch; MS, main shade (khaki); CS, contrast shade (1, blue; 2, yellow; 3, lilac; 4, rose; 5, green).

INSTRUCTIONS

Back
With 4 mm. needles and MS, cast on 130 (136) sts. K. 8 rows.
Now change to CS1 and work the foll. patt.:
Row 1: K. 10 (13), p. 1, k. 1, p. 1, k. 10, p. 1, k. 13, (p. 1, k. 1) four times, k. 13, p. 1, k. 4, p. 1, k. 2, p. 1, k. 4, p. 1, k. 14, (p. 1, k. 1) four times, k. 12, p. 1, k. 10, p. 1, k. 1, p. 1, k. 10 (13).
Row 2 : K. the k. sts. and p. the p. sts. as they face you.
When rows 1 and 2 have been worked in CS1 six times in all, change to CS2 and work rows 1 and 2 twelve times – 24 rows.

Change to MS and work rows 1 and 2 twice – 4 rows.
Change to CS3 and work rows 1 and 2 six times – 12 rows.
Change to CS4 and work rows 1 and 2 twice – 4 rows.
Change to CS1 and work rows 1 and 2 six times – 12 rows.
Change to MS and work rows 1 and 2 twice – 4 rows.
Change to CS5 and work rows 1 and 2 twelve times – 24 rows.
Change to CS2 and work rows 1 and 2 six times – 12 rows.
Change to MS and work rows 1 and 2 twice – 4 rows.
Change to CS3 and work rows 1 and 2 six times – 12 rows **.
Change to CS4 and work rows 1 and 2 six times – 12 rows.

To shape neck Still using CS4, work 49 (52), turn: work on these sts. only. Dec. 1 st. at neck edge on the next 6 rows, then cast off. Slip the centre 32 sts. onto a spare needle to be worked later as Neckband. Rejoin yarn to rem. sts. and complete other side of neck to match.

Front
Exactly as Back to **. Change to CS4 and work rows 1 and 2 twice.

To shape neck Still using CS4, work 53 (56), turn: work on these sts. only. Dec. 1 st. at neck edge on every row until 43 (46) sts. rem. When length matches Back, cast off. Slip the centre 24 sts. onto a spare needle to be worked later as Neckband. Rejoin yarn to rem. sts. and complete other side of neck to match.

Sleeves
With 4 mm. needles and MS, cast on 42 (46) sts. K. 8 rows.
Now work in st. st., working 1 inc. at each end of every foll. third row until there are 100 (110) sts. Work 10 rows straight then cast off.

TO MAKE UP

Join right shoulder seam, matching up stripes.

Neckband
With 3¾ mm. needles and CS4, pick up and k. 15 sts. along left front neck, k. across the 24 sts. of front neck, pick up and k. 15 sts. along right front neck, then k. across the 32 sts. of back neck. Work in g-st. (see page 12) for 8 rows, then cast off. Join left shoulder seam and neckband. Set in sleeves. Join sleeve seams and side seams.

Vertical stripes
With right side facing and using MS and a darning needle, work up each p. channel in chain stitch, to form the vertical stripes. Press all seams.

Bodyline Tactics

Long clingy tunic relies for impact on perfect knitting and the link cables which emphasise the sleeves and front and circle the neck.

MATERIALS

15 (16, 17) 50 g. balls Pingouin 4 Pingouins in pink; a pair each 3 mm. (no. 11) and 3¾ mm. (no. 9) knitting needles; a cable needle.

TENSION

25 stitches and 30 rows to 10 cm. over stocking stitch, using 3¾ mm. needles.

MEASUREMENTS

To fit bust 34 (36, 38) in., 86 (91, 97) cm.
Length (all sizes) approx. 30½ in., 78 cm. (excluding cable strip at neck)
Sleeve seam (all sizes) approx. 17 in., 43 cm.

ABBREVIATIONS

k., knit; p., purl; st(s)., stitch(es); beg., beginning; cont., continue; C4B, slip next 4 sts. onto cable needle and place at back of work, k. 4, then k. 4 from cable needle; C4F, slip next 4 sts. onto cable needle and place at front of work, k. 4, then k. 4 from cable needle; foll., following; inc(s)., increase(s); patt., pattern; rem., remain(ing); rep., repeat; s.k.p.o., slip one, knit one, pass slip stitch over; tog., together.

INSTRUCTIONS

Back and front (*both alike*)
With 3 mm. needles, cast on 134 (142, 150) sts. Work in k. 2, p. 2 rib for 7 cm., working 6 incs. along last rib row thus: Rib 64 (68, 72), inc. in next 6 sts., rib to end – 140 (148, 156) sts.
Change to 3¾ mm. needles and work in link cable patt. thus:
Row 1: K. 60 (64, 68), p. 2, k. 16, p. 2, k. 60 (64, 68).
Row 2: K. the k. sts. and p. the p. sts.
Rows 3 to 6: Rep. rows 1 and 2 twice more.
Row 7: K. 60 (64, 68), p. 2, C4B, C4F, p.

2, k. 60 (64, 68).
Row 8: As row 2.
Rows 9 and 10: As rows 1 and 2.
These 10 rows form patt. Cont. in patt. until work measures approx. 60 cm. from beg., ending with a row 8 of patt.

To shape raglans Cast off 8 sts. at beg. of next 2 rows – 124 (132, 140) sts.
Keeping link cable patt. on centre 80 (88, 96) sts. correct, work inverted cable patt. at each side, while shaping raglan thus:
Row 1: P. 2, k. 16, p. 2, s.k.p.o., patt. to last 22 sts., k. 2 tog., p. 2, k. 16, p. 2.
Row 2: K. the k. sts. and p. the p. sts.
Rows 3 to 6: Rep. rows 1 and 2 twice more.
Row 7: P. 2, C4F, C4B, p. 2, s.k.p.o., patt. to last 22 sts., k. 2 tog., p. 2, C4F, C4B, p. 2.
Row 8: As row 2.
Rows 9 and 10: As rows 1 and 2.
Cont. to rep. last 10 rows while keeping link cable correct in centre until 74 (82, 90) sts. rem., working p. 2 tog. eight times over each cable on last wrong side row – 50 (58, 66) sts. Cast off.

Sleeves
With 3 mm. needles, cast on 58 (62, 66) sts. Work in k. 2, p. 2 rib for 8 cm., working 20 incs. evenly along last rib row – 78 (82, 86) sts.
Change to 3¾ mm. needles and work cable patt. as for Back, set as follows:
Row 1: K. 29 (31, 33), p. 2, k. 16, p. 2, k. 29 (31, 33).
Keeping patt. correct, inc. 1 st. at each end of every foll. tenth row until there are 98 (102, 106) sts. – length 43 cm.

To shape raglan top Cast off 8 sts. at beg. of next 2 rows – 82 (86, 90) sts.
Next row: K. 2, s.k.p.o., patt. to last 4 sts., k. 2 tog., k. 2.

Next row: K. the k. sts. and p. the p. sts.
Rep. these 2 rows until 34 (38, 42) sts. rem., working p. 2 tog. eight times over centre cable on last wrong side row – 26 (30, 34) sts. Cast off.

Cable strip for neck
With 3¾ mm. needles, cast on 22 sts. Work in cable patt. as follows:
Row 1: P. 3, k. 16, p. 3.
Row 2: K. the k. sts. and p. the p. sts.
Rows 3 to 6: Rep. rows 1 and 2 twice more.
Row 7: P. 3, C4F, C4B, p. 3.
Row 8: As row 2.
Rows 9 and 10: As rows 1 and 2.
These 10 rows form patt. Rep. rows 1 to 10 sixteen times more, then rows 1 and 2 once more. Cast off.

TO MAKE UP

Press according to instructions on ball band. Join raglan seams, leaving left back raglan open. Sew cable strip to neck.

Neckband
With 3 mm. needles, pick up and k. 124 sts. along cable strip at neck. Work in k. 2, p. 2 rib for 8 cm. Cast off ribwise. Join left back raglan seam and neckband. Fold neckband in half to wrong side and sew in position. Join side and sleeve seams.

Saddle Tramp

MATERIALS

12 (14) 50 g. balls Hayfield Gaucho in main shade (shade 46003) and 1 (1) ball in each of 2 contrast shades (46006 and 46004); a pair each 5 mm. (no. 6) and 6 mm. (no. 4) knitting needles; five buttons.

TENSION

8 stitches and 9 rows to 5 cm. over stocking stitch, using 6 mm. needles.

MEASUREMENTS

To fit bust 34-36 (38-40) in., 87-92 (97-102) cm. loosely.
Length 22½ (23½) in., 57 (59) cm.
Sleeve (both sizes) 16½ in., 42 cm.

ABBREVIATIONS

k., knit; p., purl; st(s)., stitch(es); alt., alternate; beg., beginning; cont., continue; dec., decrease; foll., following; inc., increas(e)(ing); patt., pattern; rem., remain(ing); rep., repeat; st. st., stocking stitch; MS, main shade; A, first contrast shade; B, second contrast shade.

INSTRUCTIONS

Back

With 5 mm. needles and MS, cast on 76 (84) sts. Work 15 rows in k. 1, p. 1 rib. Change to 6 mm. needles. Work in st. st. (see page 12) for 60 rows.

To shape armhole Cast off 4 sts. at beg. of next 2 rows and 3 sts. on foll. 2 rows. Dec. 1 st. at each end of next 2 alt. rows – 58 (66) sts.
Cont. in st. st. until work measures 17 (18) cm. from beg. of shaping, ending with a right side row.

To shape neck Row 1: P. 21 (25), cast off next 16 sts., p. to end. Cont. on last set of 21 (25) sts. only for first side and

leave rem. sts. on a spare needle. Dec. 1 st. at neck edge on next 4 (6) rows. Cast off rem. 17 (19) sts.
Second side: Rejoin yarn to the inner end of rem. 21 (25) sts. and complete as for first side.

Right front

With 5 mm. needles and MS, cast on 48 (52) sts. Work 5 rows in k. 1, p. 1 rib.
Buttonhole row 1 (right side): Rib 5, cast off next 2 sts., rib to end.
Buttonhole row 2: Rib to last 5 sts., cast on 2 sts., rib 5.
Rib 7 rows.
Next row: Rib 3, * inc. in next st., rib 5 (4); rep. from * four (six) times, inc. in next st., rib 4 (3) sts., turn. Cont. on these 44 (50) sts. only and leave rem. 10 sts. on a safety-pin for the Buttonhole Band.
** Change to 6 mm. needles. Cont. in patt., carrying colour not in use loosely across wrong side of work.
Row 1 (right side): K. 7 A, * 6 MS, 6 A, rep. from * twice, end with 1 A (7 MS).
Row 2: P. 1 A (7 MS), * 6 A, 6 MS; rep. from * twice, 7 A.
Rows 3 to 6: Rep. rows 1 and 2 twice.
Row 7: K. 7 MS, * 6 B, 6 MS; rep. from * twice, end with 1 MS (7 B).
Row 8: P. 1 MS (7 B), * 6 MS, 6 B; rep. from * twice, 7 MS.
Rows 9 to 12: Rep. rows 7 and 8 twice. These 12 rows form patt. Rep. 12 patt. rows four times, then row 1 again.

To shape armhole Keeping patt. correct, cast off 4 sts. at beg. of next row and 3 sts. on foll. alt. row. Dec. 1 st. at same edge on next 2 alt. rows – 35 (41) sts. Patt. 4 rows straight.

To shape neck Dec. 1 st. at neck edge on every row until 17 (19) sts. rem. Cont. straight until Front measures trame as Back to shoulder. Cast off.

Left front

With 5 mm. needles and MS, cast on 48 (52) sts. Work 14 rows in k. 1, p. 1 rib.
Next row: Rib 10, then slip these 10 sts. onto a safety-pin for Button Band, rib 4 (3). * Inc. in next st., rib 5 (4); rep. from * four (six) times, inc. in next st., rib 3 – 44 (50) sts.
Complete as for Right Front from ** but reverse each patt. row so that colours match at centre front and end with patt. row 12 before working armhole shaping.

Sleeves

With 5 mm. needles and MS, cast on 42 (46) sts. Work 14 rows in k. 1, p. 1 rib.
Inc. row: Rib 4 (3), * inc. in next st., rib 10 (7); rep. from * two (four) times, inc. in next st., rib 4 (2) – 46 (52) sts.
Change to 6 mm. needles. Cont. in st. st., inc. 1 st. at each end of eleventh and each foll. twelfth row until there are 54 (60) sts. Cont. straight until the sleeve measures 42 cm. from cast on edge.

To shape top Cast off 4 sts. at beg. of next 2 rows and 2 sts. on foll. 2 rows. Dec. 1 st. at each end of every alt. row until 16 sts. rem. Cast off 3 sts. at beg. of next 2 rows. Cast off rem. 10 sts.

Button band

With 5 mm. needles and right side facing and with MS, rejoin yarn to inner end of 10 sts. on safety-pin on Left Front. Cont. in rib until band, when slightly stretched, fits up Left Front to beg. of neck shaping. Cast off ribwise. Sew in place. With pins, mark positions for 5 buttons on Button Band: the first level with buttonhole in rib at lower edge of Right Front, the fifth 4 rows from cast-off edge and the rem. three spaced evenly between.

Buttonhole band

Work as for Button Band, working buttonholes as before at pin positions.

Collar

With 5 mm. needles and MS, cast on 61 sts.
Row 1 (right side): K. 1, * p. 1, k. 1; rep. from * to end. With rib as set, cast on 4 sts. at beg. of next 4 (6) rows and 6 sts. at

Chunky warm jacket has boldly fair isled squares on the front.

beg. of next 6 rows – 113 (121) sts. Rib 16 rows. Cast off 6 sts. at beg. of next 6 rows and 4 sts. on foll. 4 (6) rows. Cast off rem. 61 sts. ribwise.

TO MAKE UP

Press as instructed on ball band, omitting rib. Join shoulder seams. Set in sleeves. Join side and sleeve seams. Beg. and ending at top of front bands, place right side of collar to right side of jacket. Sew in place. Fold collar in half onto wrong side and sew in place, joining row ends of the straight rows at centre of collar to top of front bands. Sew on buttons. Press seams.

Manor Born

MATERIALS

18 (19, 20) 50 g. balls Hayfield Grampian Chunky; a pair each 4½ mm. (no. 7) and 5 mm. (no. 6) knitting needles; a cable needle; a stitch-holder; eight buttons.

TENSION

16 stitches and 24 rows to 10 cm. over stocking stitch, using 4½ mm. needles.

MEASUREMENTS

To fit bust 34 (36, 38) in., 86 (91, 97) cm.
Side seam (all sizes) 18 in., 46 cm.
Length 25½ (26, 26½) in., 65 (66, 67) cm.
Sleeve seam (all sizes) 16¾ in., 42.5 cm.

ABBREVIATIONS

k., knit; p., purl; st(s)., stitch(es); alt., alternate; beg., beginning; cont., continue; C10B, slip next 5 sts. onto cable needle and place at back of work, k. 5, then k. 5 from cable needle; dec., decreas(e)(ing); foll., following; inc., increase; patt., pattern; rem., remain(s)(ing); rep., repeat.

INSTRUCTIONS

Back

With 4½ mm. needles, cast on 92 (96, 100) sts. Beg. odd-numbered rows with k. 2 (p. 2, k. 2) and even-numbered rows with p. 2 (k. 2, p. 2), work 16 rows in k. 2, p. 2 rib.
Change to 5 mm. needles and work patt. as follows:
Row 1: K. 18 (20, 22), p. 2, k. 10, p. 2, k. 28, p. 2, k. 10, p. 2, k. to end.
Row 2: P. 18 (20, 22), k. 2, p. 10, k. 2, p. 28, k. 2, p. 10, k. 2, p. to end.
Rows 3 to 6: Rep. rows 1 and 2 twice.
Row 7: K. 18 (20, 22), p. 2, C10B, p. 2, k. 28, p. 2, C10B, p. 2, k. to end.
Row 8: As row 2.

Long line sporty jacket with a stand-up double rib collar, saddle shoulder line and cables.

Rows 9 to 16: Rep. rows 1 and 2 four times.
These 16 rows form patt. Work patt. five times more.

To shape armholes Dec. 1 st. at beg. of next 16 (18, 20) rows – 76 (78, 80) sts. Patt. 14 rows.
Dec. 1 st. at each end of next 14 rows – 48 (50, 52) sts.

To slope the shoulders Cast off 12 sts. at beg. of next 2 rows – 24 (26, 28) sts. Leave these sts. on a spare needle.

Pocket linings *(two)*

With 5 mm. needles, cast on 30 sts.
Row 1: K. 8, p. 2, k. 10, p. 2, k. 8.
Row 2: P. 8, k. 2, p. 10, k. 2, p. 8.
These 2 rows set the position of patt. Keeping continuity of patt. to match Back, work a further 28 rows. Leave these sts. on a spare needle.

Left front

With 4½ mm. needles, cast on 56 (58, 60) sts.
Rib row 1: P. 0 (2, 0), * k. 2, p. 2; rep. from * until 1 st. rem., k. 1.
Rib row 2: P. 1, * k. 2, p. 2; rep. from * until 0 (2, 0) sts. rem., k. 0 (2, 0).
Rib a further 13 rows.
Next row: Rib 11 and leave these sts. on a safety-pin for Buttonhole Band, rib to end – 45 (47, 49) sts.
Change to 5 mm. needles and cont. as follows:
Row 1: K. 18 (20, 22), p. 2, k. 10, p. 2, k. to end.
Row 2: P. 13, k. 2, p. 10, k. 2, p. to end.
** These 2 rows set position of patt. Keeping continuity of patt. to match Back, work a further 28 rows.
Next (pocket) row: K. 10 (12, 14), (k. 8 here when working Right Front) – slip next 30 sts. onto a stitch-holder and

leave at front of work, then in their place patt. across 30 sts. of one pocket lining, k. to end – 45 (47, 49) sts.
Patt. a further 65 rows.

To shape armhole Dec. 1 st. at beg. (read *end* here when working Right Front) of next row, then on the 7 (8, 9) foll. alt. rows – 37 (38, 39) sts.
Patt. 15 rows (patt. 16 rows here when working Right Front), then dec. 1 st. at armhole edge on next 5 rows – 32 (33, 34) sts.

To shape neck and cont. armhole shaping Cast off 6 (7, 8) sts. at beg. of next row, then 3 sts. on the foll. alt. row, then dec. 1 st. at neck edge on the 2 foll. alt. rows, *at the same time* dec. 1 st. at armhole edge on the next 9 rows – 12 sts. Cast off.

Right front

With 4½ mm. needles, cast on 56 (58, 60) sts.
Rib row 1: K. 1, * p. 2, k. 2; rep. from * until 0 (2, 0) sts. rem., p. 0 (2, 0).
Rib row 2: K. 0 (2, 0), * p. 2, k. 2; rep. from * until 1 st. rem., p. 1.
Rib a further 4 rows.
Buttonhole row 1: Rib 5, cast off 3 sts., rib to end.
Buttonhole row 2: Rib to end, casting on 3 sts. over those cast off on previous row.
Rib a further 7 rows.
Next row: Rib 45 (47, 49), turn and leave rem. 11 sts. on a safety-pin for Buttonhole Band.
Change to 5 mm. needles and cont. as follows:
Row 1: K. 13, p. 2, k. 10, p. 2, k. to end.
Row 2: P. 18 (20, 22), k. 2, p. 10, k. 2, p. to end.
Work as Left Front from **, noting variations.

Sleeves

With 4½ mm. needles, cast on 46 sts.
Work 17 rows in rib as given for Back.
Inc. row: Rib 5, inc. 1, * rib 3, inc. 1; rep. from * until 4 sts. rem., rib 4 – 56 sts.
Change to 5 mm. needles and cont. as follows:
Row 1: K. 21, p. 2, k. 10, p. 2, k. 21.
Row 2: P. 21, k. 2, p. 10, k. 2, p. 21.

These 2 rows set the position of the patt. Keeping the continuity of patt. to match Back and taking extra sts. into the patt. as they occur, work 6 rows, then inc. 1 st. at each end of next row, then on the 3 (4, 5) foll. eighth rows – 64 (66, 68) sts. Patt. a further 53 (45, 37) rows.

To shape top Cast off 2 sts. at beg. of next 18 (20, 22) rows – 28 (26, 24) sts. Dec. 1 st. at beg. of next 2 rows – 26 (24, 22) sts.
Patt. 26 rows for shoulder extension. Leave these sts. on a spare needle.

Button band
With 4½ mm. needles and right side facing, rejoin yarn to sts. on safety-pin and rib 105 (107, 109) rows. Leave these sts. on a safety-pin.

Buttonhole band
With 4½ mm. needles and wrong side facing, rejoin yarn to sts. on safety-pin and rib 9 (11, 13) rows. Work the 2 buttonhole rows as given for Right Front, then rib 16 rows.
Rep. the last 18 rows four times, then the 2 buttonhole rows again. Rib 4 (6, 8) rows, then leave sts. on a spare needle.

Neckband
First join shoulder extensions of sleeves to shoulder shaping on Back and Fronts. With 4½ mm. needles and right side facing, rib across buttonhole band sts. already on needle, pick up and k. 10 (11, 12) sts. up right neck shaping, k. across 26 (24, 22) sts. of shoulder extension, k. across 24 (26, 28) sts. at back neck, k. across 26 (24, 22) sts. of shoulder extension, pick up and k. 10 (11, 12) sts. down left neck shaping, then rib across 11 sts. of button band – 118 sts.
Rib row 1: P. 2, * k. 2, p. 2; rep. from * to end.
Rib row 2: K. 2, * p. 2, k. 2; rep. from * to end.
Rib a further 9 rows.
Work the 2 buttonhole rows as given for Right Front, then rib 16 rows.

Work the 2 buttonhole rows again, then rib 8 rows. Cast off ribwise.

Pocket tops (two)
With 4½ mm. needles and right side facing, rejoin yarn to sts. on stitch-holder and beg. odd-numbered rows with k. 2 and even-numbered rows with p. 2, work 6 rows in k. 2, p. 2 rib. Cast off ribwise.

TO MAKE UP

Press with a warm iron over a dry cloth, avoiding cable panels. Join underarm seams, then join sleeve and side seams. Sew front bands into position, then fold neckband in half to wrong side of work and sew into place. Join row ends of neckband. Catch buttonhole edges together on neckband. Sew down pocket linings to wrong side of work, then row ends of pocket tops to right side of work. Sew on buttons.

Lace

MATERIALS

8 (9) 50 g. balls Pingouin Fil d'Ecosse in black (shade 5); a pair each 2¾ mm. (no. 12) and 3 mm. (no. 11) knitting needles.

TENSION

29 stitches and 32 rows to 10 cm. over pattern, using 3 mm. needles.

MEASUREMENTS

To fit bust 32-34 (36-38) in., 81-87 (91-97) cm.
Length 21¼ (21¾) in., 54 (55) cm.
Sleeve seam (both sizes) 15¼ in., 39 cm.

ABBREVIATIONS

k., knit; p., purl; st(s)., stitch(es); alt., alternate; beg., beginning; cont., continue; dec., decrease; foll., following; inc(s)., increase(s); patt., pattern; p.s.s.o., pass slip stitch over; p.2s.s.o., pass the 2 slip stitches over; rem., remain(ing); rep., repeat; rev. st. st., reversed stocking stitch; s.k.p.o., slip one, knit one, pass slip stitch over; sl., slip; tog., together; y.o.n., yarn over needle.

INSTRUCTIONS

Back

With 2¾ mm. needles, cast on 120 (130) sts. Work in k. 1, p. 1 rib for 6 cm., working 19 (23) incs. evenly along last rib row – 139 (153) sts.
Change to 3 mm. needles and work the foll. patt.:
Row 1 (wrong side): (K. 1, p. 5, k. 1) once (twice), * k. 3, (p. 3, k. 3) twice, k. 1, p. 5, k. 1; rep. from * to last 0 (7) sts., work 0 (k. 1, p. 5, k. 1).
Row 2: (P. 1, k. 1, y.o.n., sl. 1, k. 2 tog., p.s.s.o., y.o.n., k. 1, p. 1) once (twice), * p. 3, k. 3, y.o.n., sl. 2, k. 1, p.2s.s.o.,

Black lace sweater in fine cotton – definitely not for beginners. It's hell picking up any dropped stitches, because they tend to run like wildfire right down to the bottom of the rib.

y.o.n., k. 3, p. 4, k. 1, y.o.n., sl. 1, k. 2 tog., p.s.s.o., y.o.n., k. 1, p. 1; rep. from * to last 0 (7) sts., work 0 (p. 1, k. 1, y.o.n., sl. 1, k. 2 tog., p.s.s.o., y.o.n., k. 1, p. 1).
Row 3: (K. 1, p. 5, k. 1) once (twice), * k. 3, p. 9, k. 4, p. 5, k. 1; rep. from * to last 0 (7) sts., work 0 (k. 1, p. 5, k. 1).
Row 4: (P. 1, y.o.n., s.k.p.o., k. 1, k. 2 tog., y.o.n., p. 1) once (twice), * p. 3, k. 1, s.k.p.o., y.o.n., k. 3, y.o.n., k. 2 tog., k. 1, p. 4, y.o.n., s.k.p.o., k. 1, k. 2 tog., y.o.n., p. 1; rep. from * to last 0 (7) sts., work 0 (p. 1, y.o.n., s.k.p.o., k. 1, k. 2 tog., y.o.n., p. 1).
Rows 5, 7 and 9: As row 3.
Rows 6 and 10: As row 2.
Row 8: As row 4.
Row 11: As row 1.
Row 12: (P. 1, y.o.n., s.k.p.o., k. 1, k. 2 tog., y.o.n., p. 1) once (twice), * p. 1, s.k.p.o., y.o.n., k. 3, p. 3, k. 3, y.o.n., k. 2 tog., p. 2, y.o.n., s.k.p.o., k. 1, k. 2 tog., y.o.n., p. 1; rep. from * to last 0 (7) sts.,

work 0 (p. 1, y.o.n., s.k.p.o., k. 1, k. 2 tog., y.o.n., p. 1).
Row 13: (K. 1, p. 5, k. 1) once (twice), * k. 2, (p. 4, k. 3) twice, p. 5, k. 1; rep. from * to last 0 (7) sts., work 0 (k. 1, p. 5, k.1).
Row 14: (P. 1, k. 1, y.o.n., sl. 1, k. 2 tog., p.s.s.o., y.o.n., k. 1, p. 1) once (twice), * p. 2, k. 1, y.o.n., k. 2 tog., k. 1, p. 3, k. 1, s.k.p.o., y.o.n., k. 1, p. 3, k. 1, y.o.n., sl. 1, k. 2 tog., p.s.s.o., y.o.n., k. 1, p. 1; rep. from * to last 0 (7) sts., work 0 (p. 1, k. 1, y.o.n., sl. 1, k. 2 tog., p.s.s.o., y.o.n., k. 1, p. 1).
Rows 15 and 17: As row 13.
Row 16: As row 12.
Row 18: As row 14.
Row 19: As row 1.
Row 20: As row 12.
These 20 rows form patt. Cont. in patt. until work measures approx. 34 cm. from beg.

To shape armholes Cast off 9 (10) sts. at beg. of next 2 rows and 5 (7) sts. at beg. of foll. 2 rows. Dec. 1 st. at each end of foll. 5 alt. rows – 101 (109) sts. **. Working the 3 (7) sts. at each end of every row in rev. st. st. (see page 13), cont. in patt., keeping patt. sequence, until work measures 18 (19) cm. from beg. of armhole shaping.

To shape neck Work 29 (33), turn: work on these sts. only. Dec. 1 st. at neck edge on foll. 5 rows, then cast off. Sl. the centre 43 sts. onto a spare needle to be worked later as Neckband. Rejoin yarn and complete other side of neck to match.

Front

Exactly as Back to **. Working the 3 (7) sts. at each end of every row in rev. st. st., cont. in patt., keeping patt. sequence, until work measures 14 (15) cm. from beg. of armhole shaping.

To shape neck Work 36 (40), turn: work on these sts. only. Dec. 1 st. at neck edge on every row until 24 (28) sts. rem. When work from beg. of armhole shaping matches Back, cast off. Sl. the centre 29 sts. onto a spare needle to be worked later as Neckband. Rejoin yarn and complete other side of neck to match.

Sleeves

With 2¾ mm. needles, cast on 66 (70) sts. Work in k. 1, p. 1 rib for 6 cm., working 7 (17) incs. evenly along last rib row – 73 (87) sts.

Change to 3 mm. needles and work patt. as set for Back, but inc. 1 st. at each end of every foll. eighth row until there are 97 (111) sts., working the extra sts. in rev. st. st. Cont. until work measures approx. 39 cm. from beg., ending with a row 15 of patt.

To shape armholes Cast off 9 (10) sts. at beg of next 2 rows. Keeping patt. sequence, dec. 1 st. at each end of every foll. alt. row until 29 sts. rem. Cast off 8 sts. at beg. of next 2 rows, then cast off rem. sts.

Neck edging

Join right shoulder seam. With 2¾ mm. needles and right side facing, pick up and k. 22 sts. along left front neck, k. across the 29 sts. of front neck, pick up and k. 22 sts. along right front neck, 8 sts. along right back neck, k. across the 43 sts. of back neck, and pick up and k. 8 sts. along left back neck – 132 sts.
K. 5 rows.

Cast off with ripple edge as follows: cast off 2 sts., * sl. st. from right hand needle to left hand needle, cast on 2 sts., cast off 4 sts. Rep. from * to end.

TO MAKE UP

Press pieces (except rib) with a warm iron and a damp cloth. Join left shoulder seam and neck edging. Set in sleeves. Join sleeve seams and side seams. Press all seams.

Long Shot

Crossover-fronted, hip-hugging slinky sweater in an easy-to-knit subtle tweedy yarn.

MATERIALS

14 (15, 16) 50 g. balls Hayfield Grousemoor (shade – felbrigg); a pair each 5½ mm. (no. 5) and 6½ mm. (no. 3) knitting needles.

TENSION

26 stitches and 39 rows to 20 cm. over reversed stocking stitch, using 6½ mm. needles.

MEASUREMENTS

To fit bust 34 (36, 38) in., 86 (91, 97) cm.
Length from shoulder 31½ (32, 32½) in., 79.5 (80.5, 81.5) cm.
Sleeve seam (all sizes) 17 in., 43 cm.

ABBREVIATIONS

k., knit; p., purl; st(s)., stitch(es); alt., alternate; beg., beginning; cont., continue; dec., decreas(e)(ing); foll., following; inc(s)., increase(s); rem., remain(ing); rep., repeat; rev. st. st., reversed stocking stitch; tog., together.

INSTRUCTIONS

Right front

* With 5½ mm. needles, cast on 74 (78, 82) sts.
Rib row 1: K. 2, (p. 2, k. 2) to end.
Rib row 2: P. 2, (k. 2, p. 2) to end.
Rep. these 2 rows until work measures 15 cm., ending with a row 2.
Change to 6½ mm. needles *.
Next row (right side): Cast off 10 (12, 14) sts., p. to end.
** K. 1 row, then p. 1 row.

To shape front edge Cont. in rev. st. st. (see page 13), dec. 1 st. at end (for Left Front read 'beg.' here) of next row and at same edge on every foll. third row until 34 (36, 38) sts. rem., ending with a right side row.

(For Left Front work 1 more row here.)
To shape armhole Cont. to dec. 1 st. at front edge on every third row, cast off 5 sts. at beg. of next row and 3 sts. at beg. of foll. alt. row, then dec. 1 st. at armhole edge on the foll. 4 alt. rows.
Now work armhole edge straight but cont. to dec. 1 st. at front edge on every third row until 14 (15, 16) sts. rem.
Work straight until Front measures 18.5 (19.5, 20.5) cm. from beg. of armhole, ending with a wrong side row. Cast off **.

Left front

With 6½ mm. needles, cast on 64 (66, 68) sts. Work as given for Right Front from ** to **, noting the brackets.

Back

Work as given for Right Front from * to *.
Beg. with a p. row, work in rev. st. st. until Back measures the same as Front to armhole shaping, ending with a right side row.
To shape armholes Cast off 5 sts. at beg. of next 2 rows, and 3 sts. at beg. of foll. 2 rows. Dec. 1 st. at each end of next and the foll. 3 alt. rows – 50 (54, 58) sts. Work straight until Back is 1.5 cm. shorter than Front to shoulder, ending with a right side row.

To divide for neck Next row: K. 15 (16, 17), k. 2 tog., k. 1, turn and leave rem. sts. on a spare needle. Work on first set of sts. as follows:
*** Dec. 1 st. at neck edge on next 3 rows. Cast off rem. 14 (15, 16) sts. ***.
With wrong side facing, join yarn to inner end of sts. on spare needle, then cast off 14 (16, 18) sts., k. 2 tog., k. to end.
Complete as given for first side from *** to ***.

Sleeves

With 5½ mm. needles, cast on 38 (42, 46) sts. Work in k. 2, p. 2 rib as set for Right Front welt for 6.5 cm., working 6 incs. evenly along last rib row – 44 (48, 52) sts.
Change to 6½ mm. needles and beg. with a p. row, work in rev. st. st. and inc. 1 st. at each end of fifteenth and every foll. fourteenth row until there are 52 (56, 60) sts.
Work straight until Sleeve measures 43 cm. from cast on edge, ending with a right side row.

To shape top Cast off 5 sts. at beg. of next 2 rows. Dec. 1 st. at each end of next and every foll. alt. row until 14 sts. rem. Work 1 row. Cast off 3 sts. at beg of next 2 rows. Cast off rem. sts.

Front border

Join shoulder seams.
With 5½ mm. needles, cast on 12 sts. Work in k. 2, p. 2 rib until border, when slightly stretched, fits up right front, across back neck and down left front. Cast off.

TO MAKE UP

Do not press. Sew on front border. Set in sleeves. Join sleeve seams and side seams. Sew cast on edge of left front to top of welt on wrong side of work. Keep the ball bands for washing instructions.

Spare Rib

Easy summer sweater in stocking stitch has a softly shaped cowl collar in double rib.

MATERIALS

12 (12, 13) 50 g. balls Pingouin Typico; a pair each 3¼ mm. (no. 10) and 3¾ mm. (no. 9) knitting needles; a circular 3¼ mm. (no. 10) needle, 100 cm. long, for the collar; shirring elastic.

TENSION

22 stitches and 30 rows to 10 cm. over stocking stitch, using 3¾ mm. needles.

MEASUREMENTS

To fit bust 34 (36, 38) in., 86 (91, 97) cm.
Length from beginning of collar 19 (19½, 20½) in., 48 (50, 52) cm.
Sleeve seam (all sizes) 16½ in., 42 cm.

ABBREVIATIONS

k., knit; p., purl; st(s)., stitch(es); beg., beginning; inc., increas(e)(ing); p.s.s.o., pass slip stitch over; rem., remaining; rep., repeat; sl., slip; st. st., stocking stitch; tog., together.

INSTRUCTIONS

Back and front (*alike*)
With 3¼ mm. needles, cast on 92 (98, 104) sts.
Rib row 1: K. 1 (2, 1), * p. 2, k. 2; rep. from * to last 3 (4, 3) sts., p. 2, k. 1 (2, 1).
Rib row 2: P. 1 (2, 1), * k. 2, p. 2; rep. from * to last 3 (4, 3) sts., k. 2, p. 1 (2, 1).
Rep. these 2 rows fourteen times more, inc. 12 sts. evenly across last row – 104 (110, 116) sts.

Change to 3¾ mm. needles and work in st. st. (see page 12) until work measures 37 (39, 41) cm. from beg., ending with a p. row.
To shape raglan Cast off 6 sts. at beg. of next 2 rows.
Next row: K. 2, sl. 1, k. 1, p.s.s.o., k. to last 4 sts., k. 2 tog., k. 2.
Next row: P.
Rep. these 2 rows fourteen times more. Leave rem. 62 (68, 74) sts. on a spare needle.

Sleeves

With 3¼ mm. needles, cast on 72 (78, 84) sts. Rib 17 rows as Back.
Inc. row: Rib 4 (7, 10), * inc. into next st., rib 8; rep. from * to last 5 (8, 11) sts., inc. into next st., rib to end – 80 (86, 92) sts.
Change to 3¾ mm. needles and cont. in st. st. until work measures 42 cm. from beg., ending with a p. row.
To shape raglan Cast off 6 sts. at beg. of next 2 rows.
Next row: K. 2, sl. 1, k. 1, p.s.s.o., k. to last 4 sts., k. 2 tog., k. 2.
Next row: P.
Next row: K.
Next row: P.
Rep. the last 4 rows six times, then the first two of these rows again. Leave rem. 52 (58, 64) sts. on a spare needle.

Ribbed collar

With 3¼ mm. circular needle and right side facing, k. across the 62 (68, 74) sts. of back, 52 (58, 64) sts. of left sleeve, 62 (68, 74) sts. of front and 52 (58, 64) sts. of right sleeve – 228 (252, 276) sts.
Work in rounds of k. 2, p. 2 rib until collar measures 20 cm. Cast off loosely ribwise.

TO MAKE UP

Join raglan seams. Join side and sleeve seams. On wrong side of sleeves, thread several rows of shirring elastic through rib at cuff. Draw up to fit and secure ends.

Flirt

MATERIALS

9 (9, 10) 20 g. balls Jaeger Angora Spun in white (shade 550); a pair 3¼ mm. (no. 10) knitting needles; 20 (20, 22) pearl buttons.

TENSION

36 stitches and 34 rows to 10 cm. over rib.

MEASUREMENTS

To fit bust 34 (36, 38) in., 86 (91, 97) cm.
Length 20½ (21, 21½) in., 52 (53, 54) cm.

ABBREVIATIONS

k., knit; p., purl; st(s)., stitch(es); beg., beginning; cont., continue; rem., remaining; rep., repeat.

Ribby angora sweater with plunging front and back and tiny pearl buttons to fasten each shoulder edge.
Easy

INSTRUCTIONS

Back

Cast on 162 (170, 178) sts. and work in rib as follows:
Row 1: * P. 2, k. 2; rep. from * to last 2 sts., p. 2.
Row 2: * K. 2, p. 2; rep. from * to last 2 sts., k. 2.
Rep. these 2 rows until work measures 28 cm., ending with a row 2.

To divide for neck Rib 80 (84, 88) sts., turn and leave rem. sts. on a spare needle **.
Cont. on these 80 (84, 88) sts. for first side until work measures 52 (53, 54) cm. from beg. Cast off ribwise.
Rejoin yarn to rem. sts., cast off 2 sts., rib to end.

Finish to match first side. Cast off ribwise.

Front

Work as for Back to **.
Cont. on these 80 (84, 88) sts. for first side until work measures 51 (52, 53) cm. from beg., ending with a row 2.
Next row (buttonhole row): P. 2, cast off 2 sts., work a further 9 (9, 10) buttonholes, each spaced 6 sts. apart, to last 4 (8, 4) sts., rib to end.
Next row: Rib, casting on 2 sts. over those cast off on previous row. Cast off ribwise.
Rejoin yarn to rem. sts., cast off 2 sts., rib to end.
Finish to match first side, reversing buttonhole row. Cast off ribwise.

TO MAKE UP

Join side seams for 31 cm., leaving 21 (22, 23) cm. open for armhole. Sew buttons on back shoulders to correspond with buttonholes.

Sunny

MATERIALS

16 (17) 50 g. balls Pingouin Coton Naturel 8 Fils in yellow *or* 9 (10) 50 g. balls Pingouin Mohair 70; a pair each 3¾ mm. (no. 9) and 4 mm. (no. 8) knitting needles; a circular 4 mm. (no. 8) needle for working garment in one piece; a circular 3¾ mm. (no. 9) needle for neckband; a cable needle.

TENSION

26 stitches and 23 rows to 10 cm. over pattern, using 4 mm. needles.

MEASUREMENTS

To fit bust 32-34 (36-38) in., 81-86 (91-97) cm.
Full length (both sizes) 24½ in., 62 cm.
Sleeve seam (both sizes) 16½ in., 42 cm.

ABBREVIATIONS

k., knit; p., purl; st(s)., stitch(es); beg., beginning; cont., continue; C6B, slip next 3 sts. onto cable needle and place at back of work, k. 3, then k. 3 from cable needle; C6F, slip next 3 sts. onto cable needle and place at front of work, k. 3, then k. 3 from cable needle; dec., decrease; inc., increase; m. 1, pick up loop which lies between sts. and k. into back of it; patt., pattern; rem., remain(ing); rep., repeat; s.s.k., slip 1st and 2nd sts. knitwise from left hand needle, then insert the tip of left hand needle into the front of these 2 sts. and k. them tog.; tog., together; y.o.n., yarn over needle.

INSTRUCTIONS

Worked in one piece (starting at lower front edge).
With 3¾ mm. needles, cast on 110 (122) sts. Work in k. 1, p. 1 rib for 16 rows.
Next row: Rib 7, * m. 1, rib 6; rep. from * to last st., rib 1 – 127 (141) sts.

Dolman-sleeved cotton sweater knitted all in one piece in lace and cable pattern, with a low round neck.

Change to 4 mm. needles and work in patt. as follows:
Row 1 and every odd row (wrong side): K. 1, * p. 2 tog., y.o.n., p. 11, k. 1; rep. from * to end.
Row 2: K. 1, * s.s.k., y.o.n., C6B, k. 6; rep. from * to end.
Row 4: K. 1, * s.s.k., y.o.n., k. 12; rep. from * to end.
Row 6: K. 1, * s.s.k., y.o.n., k. 3, C6F, k. 3; rep. from * to end.
Row 8: As row 4.
These 8 rows form patt. Cont. in patt. until work measures 38 cm. from beg. and row 6 of twelfth patt. rep. has been completed.

To shape sleeves With 4 mm. circular needle and working in rows, inc. 1 st. at each end of next 14 rows, taking extra sts. into patt. – 155 (169) sts.
Cast on 14 sts. at beg. of next 2 rows – 183 (197) sts.
Cast on 28 sts. at beg. of next 4 rows – 295 (309) sts.
Work straight in patt. until straight edge of sleeve measures 14 (15) cm. and eighteenth patt. rep. has been completed.

To shape neck Patt. 126 (133) sts., turn: cont. on these sts. only. Dec. 1 st. at neck edge on every row until 114 (121) sts. rem. Work 4 rows straight, ending with row 8 of twenty-first patt. rep. Place a marker at each end of this row, inc. 1 st. at neck edge on next 6 rows. Slip centre 43 sts. onto a spare needle. Rejoin yarn to rem. 126 (133) sts. and complete other side of neck to match.
Cast on 55 sts. at neck edge and cont. in patt., working over all sts. until Back matches Front from marked point.

To shape back sleeves Cast off 28 sts. at beg. of next 4 rows – 183 (197) sts.
Cast off 14 sts. at beg. of next 2 rows – 155 (169) sts.

Dec. 1 st. at each end of next 14 rows – 127 (141) sts.
Cont. until Back matches Front to ribbing, ending with a wrong side row.
Next row: Rib 7, * work 2 tog., rib 5; rep. from * to last st., rib 1.
Work 16 rows in rib. Cast off ribwise.

Neckband

With 3¼ mm. circular needle, k. up 52 sts. across back neck edge, 11 sts. down left front neck edge, k. 7 sts. from centre, then k. 2 tog. fifteen times, k. rem. 6 sts. from centre, k. 11 sts. up right front neck edge – 102 sts.
Work in rounds of k. 1, p. 1 rib for 8 rounds. Cast off ribwise.

Cuffs

With 3¾ mm. needles and right side facing, k. up 73 sts. along sleeve edge.
Dec. row: P. 1, * p. 2 tog.; rep. from * to last st., p. 1 – 49 sts.
Work in k. 1, p. 1 rib for 14 rows. Cast off ribwise.
Work other cuff to match.

TO MAKE UP

Join side seams. Join sleeve seams and cuffs. Press all seams.

Appeal Against The Light

MATERIALS

13 (14, 15) 50 g. balls Pingouin Coton Naturel 8 Fils in main shade and 1 (1, 1) ball in each of 2 contrast shades; a pair each 3¼ mm. (no. 10) and 4 mm. (no. 8) knitting needles; a cable needle; a circular 3¼ mm. (no. 10) needle for front band; four buttons.

TENSION

20 stitches and 26 rows to 10 cm. over stocking stitch, using 4 mm. needles.

MEASUREMENTS

To fit bust 34 (36, 38) in., 86 (91, 96) cm.
Length 22¾ (23½, 24¼) in., 58 (60, 61) cm.
Sleeve seam (all sizes) 17 in., 43 cm.

ABBREVIATIONS

k., knit; p., purl; st(s)., stitch(es); alt., alternate; beg., beginning; cont., continue; C10F, slip next 5 sts. onto cable needle and place at front of work, k. 5, then k. 5 from cable needle; dec(s)., decrease(s); foll., following; inc(s)., increase(s); m. 1, pick up st. lying between needles and k. into back of it; patt., pattern; rem., remain(ing); rep., repeat; MS, main shade; CS1, first contrast shade; CS2, second contrast shade.

INSTRUCTIONS

Back

With 3¼ mm. needles and MS, cast on 108 (112, 116) sts. Work in k. 1, p. 1 rib for 8 rows.
Change to CS1 and work in k. 1, p. 1 rib for 2 rows.
Break CS1 and with MS work in k. 1, p. 1 rib for 4 rows.
Change to CS2 and work in k. 1, p. 1 rib for 2 rows.
Break CS2 and with MS work in k. 1, p. 1

rib for 5 rows.
Inc. row: (Rib 10, m. 1) to last 8 (12, 16) sts., rib 8 (12, 16) – 118 (122, 126) sts. Change to 4 mm. needles and work the foll. cable patt.:
Row 1 (right side): P. 20 (22, 24), k. 2, p. 4, k. 10, p. 4, k. 2, p. 34, k. 2, p. 4, k. 10, p. 4, k. 2, p. 20 (22, 24).
Row 2: K. 20 (22, 24), p. 2, k. 4, p. 10, k. 4, p. 2, k. 34, p. 2, k. 4, p. 10, k. 4, p. 2, k. 20 (22, 24).
Rows 3 to 6: Rep. rows 1 and 2 twice more.
Row 7: P. 20 (22, 24), k. 2, p. 4, C10F, p. 4, k. 2, p. 34, k. 2, p. 4, C10F, p. 4, k. 2, p. 20 (22, 24).
Row 8: As row 2.
Rows 9 to 14: Rep. rows 1 and 2 three times more.
These 14 rows form patt. Work straight until Back measures 38 cm. from beg., ending with a wrong side row.

To shape armholes Cast off 6 sts. at beg. of next 2 rows, 4 sts. at beg. of foll. 2 rows, then dec. 1 st. at each end of foll. 4 alt. rows – 90 (94, 98) sts.
Work straight until armholes measure 18 (19, 20) cm.

To shape neck Work 30 (32, 34), cast off centre 30 sts., work to end. Finish each side sep. Dec. 1 st. at neck edge on every row until 26 sts. rem., working 3 decs. over cable on last row – 23 sts. Cast off. Rejoin yarn and complete other side of neck to match.

Left front

With 3¼ mm. needles and MS, cast on 50 (52, 54) sts. Work 8 rows in k. 1, p. 1 rib. Complete stripes in rib as set for Back, until 21 rib rows have been worked.
Inc. row: Work 5 incs. evenly along next rib row – 55 (57, 59) sts.
Change to 4 mm. needles and work cable patt. as set for Back as follows:
Row 1: P. 20 (22, 24), k. 2, p. 4, k. 10, p. 4, k. 2, p. 13.
Row 2: K. 13, p. 2, k. 4, p. 10, k. 4, p. 2, k. 20 (22, 24).
When work measures 36 cm. from beg., shape neck by dec. 1 st. at neck edge on next and every foll. third row. When

work measures 38 cm. from beg., shape armhole as follows:

To shape armhole Cont. to dec. at neck edge as before, *at the same time*, at armhole edge, cast off 6 sts., then 4 sts. on foll. alt. row. Now dec. 1 st. at armhole edge on foll. 4 alt. rows. Cont. to shape neck as set to 26 sts., and when length from beg. of armhole matches that of Back, work 5 decs. over cable on last row – 23 sts. Cast off.

Right front

As Left Front, reversing all shapings and patt. rows.
Row 1 will read: P. 13, k. 2, p. 4, k. 10, p. 4, k. 2, p. 20 (22, 24).

Sleeves

With 3¼ mm. needles and MS, cast on 54 (58, 62) sts. and work rib and stripes as set for Back, until fifth rib row in MS has been completed after the CS2 stripe.
Inc. row: Rib 7 (9, 11), * inc. in next st., rib 2; rep. from * to last 5 (7, 9) sts., rib to end – 68 (72, 76) sts.
Change to 4 mm. needles and work cable patt. as set for Back.
Row 1: P. 23 (25, 27), k. 2, p. 4, k. 10, p. 4, k. 2, p. 23 (25, 27).
Row 2: K. 23 (25, 27), p. 2, k. 4, p. 10, k. 4, p. 2, k. 23 (25, 27). When the 14 rows of patt. have been worked once, work rows 1 to 7 once more.
Now cont. in patt. but inc. 1 st. at each end of next and every foll. eighth row until there are 84 (88, 92) sts. and work measures 43 cm. from beg.

To shape armhole Cast off 6 sts. at beg. of next 2 rows, then 4 sts. at beg. of foll. 2 rows. Dec. 1 st. at each end of every alt. row until 32 sts. rem. Cast off 6 sts. at beg. of next 2 rows. Cast off rem. sts. Join shoulder seams.

Front bands

With 3¼ mm. circular needle and right side facing and with MS, beg. at right front bottom edge, pick up and k. 74 sts. up right front edge, 52 (52, 54) sts. along right neck edge, 50 (52, 54) sts. along back neck edge, 52 (52, 54) sts. along left neck edge and 74 sts. along left front edge. Work 3 rows in k. 1, p. 1 rib.
Change to CS1 and work 2 rows in k. 1, p. 1 rib.
Break CS1 and change to MS. Work 2 rows in k. 1, p. 1 rib.
Buttonhole row: Rib 8, (cast off 3 sts., rib 17, including st. used in casting off) three times, cast off 3 sts., rib to end.
Next row: Rib, but cast on 3 sts. in place of cast off sts., for all four buttonholes. Change to CS2 and work 2 rows in rib. Break CS2 and with MS rib 2 more rows, then cast off ribwise.

TO MAKE UP

Set in sleeves. Join sleeve seams and side seams. Sew on buttons.

Classic cricket cardigan in cotton with striped bands and cabling.
Easy

Tricot Treat

MATERIALS

10 (11, 12) 25 g. balls Hayfield Aspen Mohair in main shade – mulberry (shade 53 001), 4 (5, 5) balls in first contrast shade – burgundy (53 017) and 1 (1, 1) ball in each of 2 further contrast shades – raspberry (53 011) and heather (53 015); a pair each 4½ mm. (no. 7) and 5 mm. (no. 6) knitting needles.

TENSION

17 stitches and 20 rows to 10 cm. over stocking stitch, using 5 mm. needles.

MEASUREMENTS

To fit bust 34 (36, 38) in., 87 (92, 97) cm.
Length 23 (23½, 24) in., 59 (60, 61) cm.
Sleeve seam (all sizes) 17 in., 43 cm.

ABBREVIATIONS

k., knit; p., purl; st(s)., stitch(es); alt., alternate; beg., beginning; cont., continue; dec., decrease; foll., following; inc(s)., increase(s); patt., pattern; rem., remain(ing); sep., separately; st. st., stocking stitch; MS, main shade (mulberry); CS1, first contrast shade (burgundy); CS2, second contrast shade (raspberry); CS3, third contrast shade (heather).

NOTE

See page 10 for information on reading a chart.

INSTRUCTIONS

Back

With 4½ mm. needles and MS, cast on 81 (85, 89) sts. Work in k. 1, p. 1 rib (beg. alt. rows p. 1) for 7 cm., working 5 incs. evenly along last rib row – 86 (90, 94) sts.
Change to 5 mm. needles and CS1 and work 4 rows in st. st. (see page 12).

Stripy sweater in mauve and burgundy with a jokey trompe l'oeil scarf.

Change to MS and work 8 rows in st. st. These 12 rows form stripe patt. which is worked throughout and as background to scarf *.
When stripe patt. has been worked five times, change to CS1 and work 4 rows in st. st., keeping stripe patt. as set.

To shape armholes Cast off 6 sts. at beg. of next 2 rows and 3 sts. at beg. of foll. 2 rows. Dec. 1 st. at the end of the next alt. row – 66 (70, 74) sts.
Cont. to work stripe patt. until 24 rows have been completed from the beg. of armhole shaping. Now work fair isle from Chart 1 until row 12 has been completed. Cont. as given on Chart and shape neck.

To shape neck Work 22 (24, 26) sts., turn: finish each side sep. Dec. 1 st. at neck edge on every row until 16 (18, 20) sts. rem. Work 0 (2, 4) rows straight. Cast off. Slip the centre 22 sts. onto a spare needle to be worked later as Neckband. Rejoin yarn and complete other side of neck to match.

Front

Exactly as Back to *.
When stripe patt. has been worked three times, change to CS1 and work 4 rows in st. st., then change to MS and work 2 rows in st. st. Cont. to work stripes as background, but now work fair isle from Chart 2 until row 22 has been completed.

To shape armholes Cast off 6 sts. at beg. of next 2 rows and 3 sts. at beg. of foll. 2 rows. Dec. 1 st. at each end of the foll. alt. row – 66 (70, 74) sts.
Cont. to work from Chart until row 54 has been completed.

To shape neck Work 24 (26, 28), slip next 18 sts. onto a spare needle to be

worked later as Neckband. Finish each side sep. Dec. 1 st. at neck edge on every row until 16 (18, 20) sts. rem. When length from beg. of armhole matches that of Back, cast off. Rejoin yarn and complete other side of neck to match.

Sleeves

With 4½ mm. needles and MS, cast on 41 (45, 49) sts. Work in k. 1, p. 1 rib (beg. alt. rows p. 1) for 6 cm., working 7 incs. evenly along last rib row – 48 (52, 56) sts.
Change to 5 mm. needles and work stripe patt. as set for Back, *at the same time* inc. 1 st. at each end of first and every foll. eighth row until there are 64 (68, 72) sts.
When the sixth stripe in CS1 has been completed, change to MS and work 6 rows in st. st.

To shape top Cont. in stripe patt. as before. Cast off 6 sts. at beg. of next 2 rows and 3 sts. at beg. of foll. 2 rows. Dec. 1 st. at each end of every foll. alt. row until 26 sts. rem. Cast off 6 sts. at beg. of next 2 rows. Cast off rem. sts.

Neckband

Join right shoulder seam.
With 5 mm. needles and MS, pick up and k. 11 sts. along left neck edge, k. across the 18 sts. of front neck, pick up and k. 11 sts. along right front neck, 8 sts. along right back neck, k. across the 22 sts. of back centre neck and pick up and k. 8 sts. along left back neck – 78 sts.
Work in k. 1, p. 1 rib for 14 rows, then cast off ribwise.

TO MAKE UP

Join left shoulder seam and neckband. Fold neckband in half and stitch down on the inside. Set in sleeves. Join sleeve seams and side seams, matching up stripes.

Tricot Treat

Chart 1

This is the correct number of sts. for 1st size.
For 2nd and 3rd sizes, work an extra 2 (4) sts. at each end of every row.

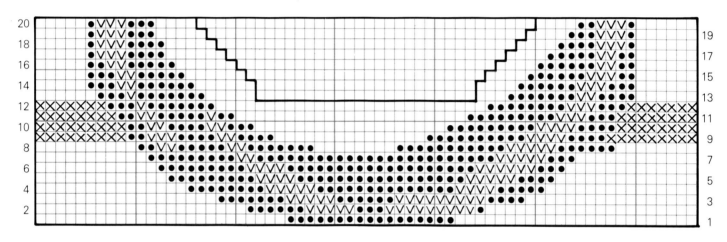

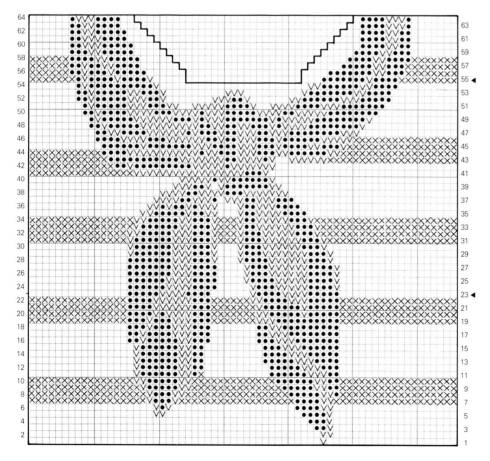

Chart 2

Shape neck ◀

This is the correct number of sts. for 1st size. After armhole shaping, cont. to work an extra 2 (4) sts. at each end of every row for 2nd and 3rd sizes.

For rows 1 to 22, work 10 (12, 14) sts. in st. st. (in stripe sequence) at each end of every row.

Shape armhole ◀

KEY
Hayfield Aspen Mohair

☐ main shade (MS), mulberry (no. 53 001)
V (CS2), raspberry (no. 53 011)
● (CS3), heather (no. 53 015)
✕ (CS1), burgundy (no. 53 017)

Note: Read odd-numbered (k.) rows from right to left and even-numbered (p.) rows from left to right.

Just Checking

Sophisticated jacket in bold checks. The vertical lines are crocheted in afterwards, or can be worked in chain stitch with a darning needle.

MATERIALS

12 (12, 13) 50 g. balls Patons Clansman D.K. in black and 4 (4, 4) balls in white; a pair each 3¼ mm. (no. 10) and 3¾ mm. (no. 9) knitting needles; a 3 mm. (no. 11) crochet hook or a darning needle; two shoulder pads (optional); seven buttons.

TENSION

25 stitches and 30 rows to 10 cm. over stocking stitch, using 3¾ mm. needles.

NOTE

As the design is meant to resemble fabric, the work must be knitted firmly, and it is therefore *essential* to work to the stated tension.

MEASUREMENTS

To fit bust 34 (36, 38) in., 86 (91, 97) cm.
Length 24½ (24½, 25) in., 62 (62, 63) cm.
Sleeve (all sizes) 17 in., 43 cm.

ABBREVIATIONS

k., knit; p., purl; st(s)., stitch(es); alt., alternate; beg., beginning; cont., continue; dec., decreas(e)(ing); foll., following; inc., increas(e)(ing); patt., pattern; rem., remain(ing); rep., repeat; sep., separately; st. st., stocking stitch; t.b.l., through back of loop; tog., together; MS, main shade (black); CS, contrast shade (white).

Just Checking

INSTRUCTIONS

Back

With 3¼ mm. needles and MS, cast on 127 (135, 143) sts. Beg. with a k. row, work 7 rows in st. st. (see page 12).
Next row: K. each st. t.b.l. instead of purling to form a ridge for hemline **.
Change to 3¾ mm. needles and work in patt. as follows:
Row 1: K. 8 (12, 16), * p. 1, k. 1, p. 1, k. 15 *; rep. from * to * to last 11 (15, 19) sts., p. 1, k. 1, p. 1, k. 8 (12, 16).
Row 2: P. 8 (12, 16), * k. 1, p. 1, k. 1, p. 15 *; rep. from * to * to last 11 (15, 19) sts., k. 1, p. 1, k. 1, p. 8 (12, 16).
Rows 3 to 16: Rep. rows 1 and 2 seven times.
Row 17: Change to CS and rep. row 1.
Row 18: Change to MS and rep. row 2.
Row 19: As row 17.
Row 20: As row 18.
These 20 rows form patt. Work patt. seven times in all.

To shape armholes Keeping continuity of patt., cast off 7 sts. at beg. of next 2 rows, then 4 sts. at beg. of foll. 2 rows – 105 (113, 121) sts.
Now dec. 1 st. at each end of next and every alt. row until 99 (107, 115) sts. rem. Cont. in patt. until armhole measures 18 (19, 20) cm., ending with a wrong side row.

To shape neck Patt. 35 (38, 40), cast off middle 29 (31, 35) sts., patt. to end. Finish each side sep. Dec. 1 st. at neck edge on every row until 29 (32, 34) sts. rem. Work straight until armhole measures 20 (21, 22) cm., ending with right side facing. Cast off. Rejoin yarn and complete other side to match, reversing shapings.

Right front

With 3¼ mm. needles and MS, cast on 62 (66, 70) sts. Work exactly as Back to **.
Change to 3¾ mm. needles and work patt. row 1 as follows:
Row 1: * K. 15, p. 1, k. 1, p. 1; * rep. from * to * to last 8 (12, 16) sts., k. 8 (12, 16).

Cont. in patt. as for Back. When the patt. has been completed twice, leave these sts. on a spare needle.

To work pocket lining With 3¾ mm. needles and MS, cast on 23 sts. Work in st. st. until work measures 12 cm. from beg., ending with a p. row. Do not cast off.
Return to Right Front.

To work pocket opening Work 22 (26, 30) sts. in patt. With 3¼ mm. needles, work the next 23 sts. sep. in k. 1, p. 1 rib, beg. with p. 1, for 8 rows, then cast these sts. off ribwise. Work over the 23 sts. of Pocket Lining in patt. in place of cast off sts., work in patt. to end. Cont. to work the 20 rows of patt. until the seventh patt. rep. has been completed. Work next row in patt.

To shape armhole and neck At armhole edge, cast off 7 sts., then 4 sts. on foll. alt. row. Now dec. 1 st. at same edge on foll. 3 alt. rows, *at the same time* dec. 1 st. at neck edge on next and every foll. third row until 29 (32, 34) sts. rem. When length from beg. of armhole matches that of Back, cast off.

Left front

As Right Front, reversing all shapings, and working patt. row 1 as follows:
Row 1: K. 8 (12, 16), * p. 1, k. 1, p. 1, k. 15 *; rep. from * to * to end. When working pocket opening row, work 17 sts. in patt., work the next 23 sts. in rib, work 22 (26, 30).

Sleeves

With 3¼ mm. needles, cast on 63 (71, 79) sts. Work exactly as Back to **.
Change to 3¾ mm. needles and work patt. row 1 as follows:
Row 1: K. 12 (16, 2), * p. 1, k. 1, p. 1, k. 15 *; rep. from * to * to last 15 (19, 5) sts., k. 1, p. 1, k. 1, k. 12 (16, 2).
Cont. in patt. as for Back, shaping sides by inc. 1 st. at each end of every foll. tenth row until there are 85 (93, 101) sts. and the patt. has been completed six times from beg.

To shape top Cast off 7 sts. at beg. of next 2 rows, then dec. 1 st. at each end of

next and every alt. row until 27 (29, 31) sts. rem. Work 1 row. Cast off 5 sts. at beg. of next 2 rows. Cast off rem. sts.

Front band

Join shoulders. With 3¼ mm. needles and MS, cast on 14 sts. Work 8 rows in k. 1, p. 1 rib.

Next 2 rows (to make buttonhole): Rib 6, cast off 2 sts., rib to end, and back, casting on 2 sts., over those cast off. Work 18 rows in k. 1, p. 1 rib. Work a buttonhole as before. Cont. thus until 7 buttonholes have been worked in all. Now cont. in rib without buttonholes until band fits entire inner edge. Cast off ribwise.

TO MAKE UP

Omitting ribbing, press according to instructions on ball band. With 3 mm. crochet hook and CS, work a chain up each p. st. on the right side to complete the squares; if preferred, work chain stitch with darning needle. Set in sleeves. Join sleeve seams and side seams, matching up patt. Fold hems at ridge to wrong side and slip stitch loosely in position. Sew on front band. Stitch down pocket linings. Press seams. Sew on buttons. Sew in shoulder pads if required.

Valentine

MATERIALS

9 (10) 50 g. balls Patons Clansman D.K. in main shade – light natural (shade 1379), 2 (2) balls in shell pink (7790), 1 (2) balls in water green (2632), 1 (2) balls in laburnum (7789), 1 (2) balls in beryl (7869) and 1 (1) ball in clover (2480); a pair each 3¼ mm. (no. 10) and 3¾ mm. (no. 9) knitting needles.

TENSION

25 stitches and 28 rows to 10 cm. over pattern.

MEASUREMENTS

To fit bust 34-36 (37-39) in., 86-91 (94-99) cm.
Length 24 (24½) in., 61 (62) cm.
Sleeve (both sizes) 16½ in., 42 cm.

ABBREVIATIONS

k., knit; p., purl; st(s)., stitch(es); alt., alternate; beg., beginning; cont., continue; dec., decrease; foll., following; inc., increase; patt(s)., pattern(s); rem., remain(ing); rep., repeat; st. st., stocking stitch; tog., together; MS, main shade (light natural).

NOTE

See page 10 for information on reading a chart.

INSTRUCTIONS

Back
With 3¼ mm. needles and MS, cast on 122 (132) sts. Work in k. 1, p. 1 rib for 5 cm.
Change to 3¾ mm. needles and work in patt. from Chart, knitting 1 extra st. at each end as a selvedge st. Work rows 1 to 60 once, then rows 1 to 48 once more.

To shape armholes Cast off 8 sts. at beg. of next 2 rows and 3 sts. at beg. of foll. 2 rows – 100 (110) sts.

Now dec. 1 st. at each end of every alt. row until 92 (102) sts. rem. Cont. in patt. until 2 complete patts. from beg. have been worked *, then work rows 1 to 36 once more.

To shape back neck Rep. patt. stripe by working rows 31 to 36 again, then *for*

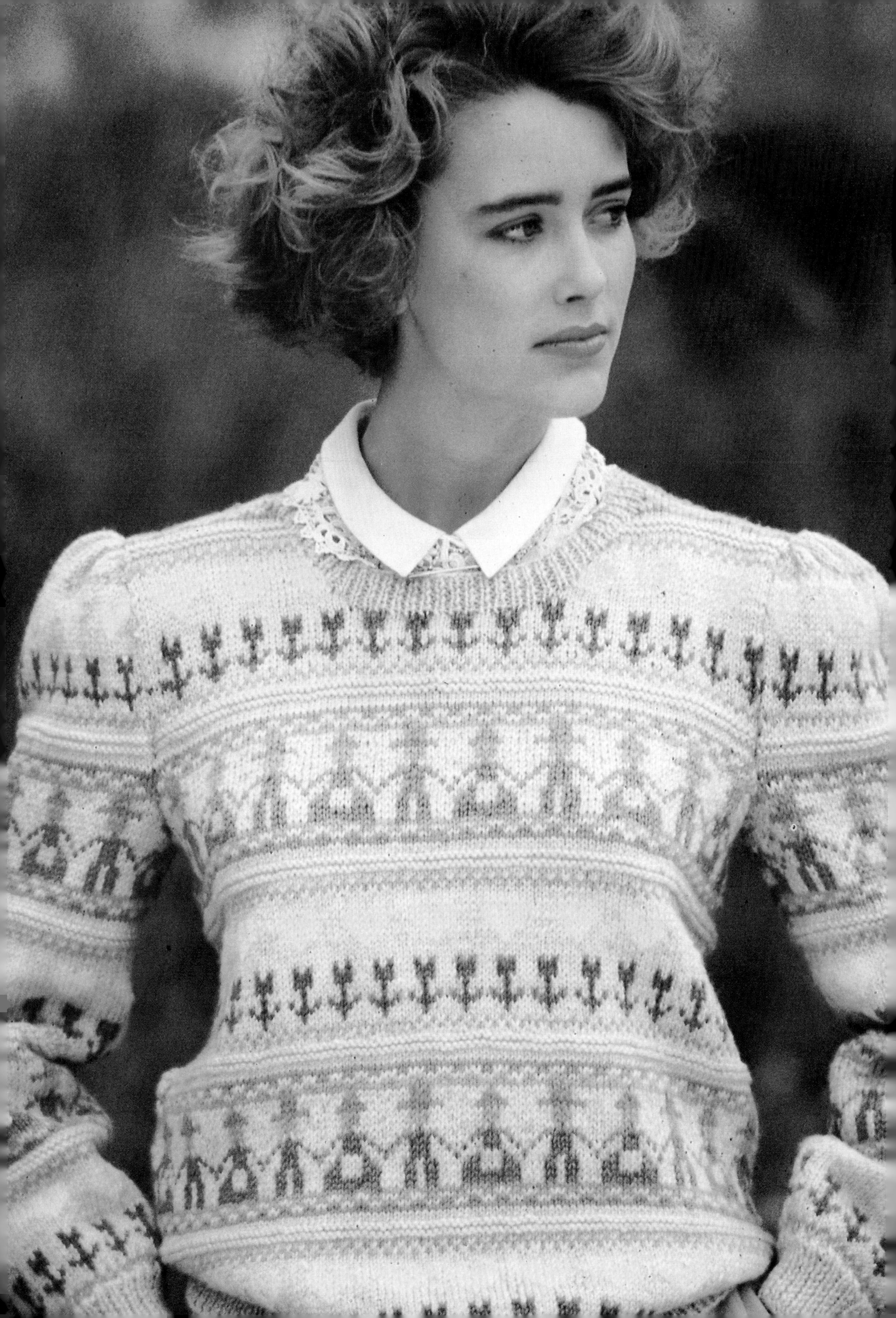

Valentine

KEY
Patons Clansman D.K.

☐ main shade, light natural (no. 1379)

✕ shell pink (no. 7790)

◯ water green (no. 2632)

╱ laburnum (no. 7789)

● main shade (no. 1379), every st. k.

■ clover (no. 2480)

⬤ beryl (no. 7869)

When working rows 5 to 12, keep repeating the first 6 sts. only, working the last 4 sts. in MS for 2nd size only.

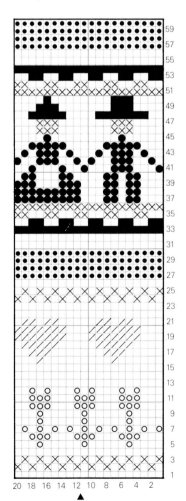

Begin 2nd size here for Back and Front and 1st size for Sleeves.

Multiple of 20 patt. sts., with 1 selvedge st. at each end of every row. Except where stated, work in st. st. Beg. 2nd size here for Back and Front, and 1st size for Sleeves.

2nd size only cont. in MS for 4 rows, but *at the same time for both sizes,* shaping neck when row 32 (36) has been worked thus:
Next row: Patt. 24 (28), k. 2 tog., turn: work on these sts. only. Dec. 1 st. at neck edge on foll. 3 rows, then cast off rem. 22 (26) sts. Return to other sts., slip the centre 40 (42) sts. onto a spare needle, rejoin yarns and work to match first side.

Front

Work as for Back to *. Now work rows 1 to 16 (20) once more.

To shape neck Next row: Keeping continuity of patt., work 31 (35) sts., k. 2 tog., turn.
Now dec. 1 st. at neck edge on every alt. row until 22 (26) sts. rem. Cont. straight until work measures as Back to shoulder. Cast off. Return to other sts., slip centre 26 (28) sts. onto a spare needle, rejoin yarns and work to match other side.

Sleeves

With 3¼ mm. needles and MS, cast on 56 (62) sts. Work in k. 1, p. 1 rib for 5 cm., inc. across last row thus:
Inc. row: (Rib 2, inc. in next st.) six times, * rib 4 (2), inc. in next st. *; rep. from * to * three (seven) times more, (rib 2, inc. in next st.) six times, then *for 2nd size only* rib 2 – 72 (82) sts.
Change to 3¾ mm. needles and work in patt. from Chart noting chart instructions, and inc. 1 st. at each end of every row 10 until there are 92 (102) sts., working inc. sts. into patt.
Cont. straight now until the same number of rows as on Back to armhole shaping have been worked.

To shape top Cast off 7 sts. at beg. of next 2 rows, and 3 sts. at beg. of foll. 2 rows, then dec. 1 st. at each end of next alt. row – 70 (80) sts.
Keeping continuity of patt., cont. straight until row 26 of the third complete patt. from beg. has been worked.
Now work in st. st. in MS only, shaping thus:
K. to last 5 sts., turn, p. to last 5 sts., turn, k. to last 10 sts., turn, p. to last 10 sts., turn. Cont. in this way, leaving 5 more

sts. at each end unworked on *every row* until 10 sts. rem. in centre, turn.
Next row: K. to end.
Next row: P. to end.
Cast off 5 sts. at beg. of next 2 rows.
Next row: K. 2 tog. to end.
Cast off rem. sts.

Neckband

Join right shoulder seam. With 3¼ mm. needles and right side facing and with MS, pick up and k. 24 (26) sts. down left front neck edge, work in k. 1, p. 1 rib over the 26 (28) centre front sts., pick up and k. 24 (26) sts. up right neck edge, 4 (8) sts. along right back neck, rib over centre 40 (42) back neck sts., and pick up and k. 4 (8) sts. along left back neck edge – 122 (138) sts.
Work in k. 1, p. 1 rib for 9 rows, then cast off ribwise.

TO MAKE UP

Press work avoiding ribbing, following instructions on ball band. Join left shoulder and neckband seam. Sew in sleeves, gathering in sleeve top slightly. Join sleeve and side seams. Lightly press seams.

Broadway Baby

MATERIALS

7 (8, 9) 25 g. balls Sirdar Wash'n'Wear Double Crepe; a pair each 3¾ mm. (no. 9) and 4 mm. (no. 8) knitting needles; 12 (14, 16) strings 8 mm. knitting sequins.

TENSION

12 stitches and 15 rows to 5 cm.

MEASUREMENTS

To fit bust 32 (34, 36) in., 81 (86, 91) cm.
Length 14 (15, 16) in., 36 (38, 40) cm.
Sleeve (all sizes) 15½ in., 40 cm.

ABBREVIATIONS

k., knit; p., purl; st(s)., stitch(es); alt., alternate; beg., beginning; cont., continue; dec., decrease; foll., following; inc., increas(e)(ing); patt., pattern; rem., remain(ing); rep., repeat; s. 1, sequin 1 (see note below); st. st., stocking stitch; t.b.l., through back of loop.

NOTE ON SEQUIN KNITTING

Before inserting needle into next st., move a sequin up close to back of work and draw sequin through centre of next st. as you knit – referred to as s. 1.

INSTRUCTIONS

Thread 2 strings of sequins onto each of 6 (7, 8) balls of yarn.

Back

With 3¾ mm. needles and unsequinned yarn, cast on 91 (97, 103) sts. Beg. with a k. row, work 7 rows in st. st. (see page 12) for hem.
K. t.b.l. 1 row.
Change to 4 mm. needles and sequinned yarn. See note on sequin knitting (above) and patt. thus:

Dazzlingly blue sequin jacket, cropped, with hems stitched down on the inside. You'll need all of that famous patience to knit the sequins; the technique is simple but fiddly.

Row 1: K. 1 t.b.l., (s. 1, k. 1 t.b.l.) to end.
Row 2: P.
Row 3: K. 1 t.b.l., (k. 1 t.b.l., s. 1) to last 2 sts., k. 2 t.b.l.
Row 4: P. *.
These 4 rows form patt. Rep. them once, then cont. in patt. and inc. 1 st. at each end of next and every foll. eighth row until there are 101 (107, 113) sts. Cont. straight until work measures 18 (19, 20) cm. from top of hem.

To shape armhole Cast off 4 sts. at beg. of next 4 rows. Dec. 1 st. at each end of next and every foll. alt. row until 79 (83, 87) sts. rem. Cont. straight until work measures 36 (38, 40) cm. from top of hem.

To shape shoulder Cast off 7 sts. at beg. of next 4 rows and 6 (7, 8) sts. at beg. of foll. 2 rows. Cast off 39 (41, 43) sts.

Left front

With 3¾ mm. needles and unsequinned yarn, cast on 41 (45, 47) sts. Beg. with a k. row and inc. 1 st. at end of first, third, fifth and seventh rows, work 7 rows in st. st. for hem – 45 (49, 51) sts.
K. t.b.l. 1 row.
Change to 4 mm. needles and sequinned yarn. Patt. 8 rows as Back. Inc. 1 st. at beg. of next and every foll. eighth row until there are 50 (54, 56) sts. Cont. until work measures 18 (19, 20) cm. from top of hem, ending at shaped edge.

To shape armhole and front Cast off 4 sts. at beg. of next and foll. alt. row, then dec. 1 st. at each end of next 3 (4, 5) alt. rows. Cont. to dec. 1 st. at front edge only on every alt. row until 20 (21, 22) sts. rem. Cont. straight until work measures 36 (38, 40) cm. from top of hem, ending at armhole.

To shape shoulder Cast off 7 sts. at beg. of next and foll. alt. row. Work 1 row. Cast off 6 (7, 8) sts.

Right front

With 3¾ mm. needles and unsequinned yarn, cast on 41 (45, 47) sts. Beg. with a k. row and inc. 1 st. at beg. of first, third, fifth and seventh rows, work 7 rows in st. st. for hem – 45 (49, 51) sts.
K. t.b.l. 1 row.
Cont. as for Left Front, reversing shapings.

Sleeves

With 3¾ mm. needles and unsequinned yarn, cast on 47 (49, 51) sts. Work as Back to *. Rep. last 4 rows once, then inc. 1 st. at each end of next and every foll. sixth row until there are 81 (85, 89) sts. Cont. straight until work measures 40 cm. from top of hem.

To shape top Cast off 4 sts. at beg. of next 4 rows. Dec. 1 st. at each end of next and every foll. alt. row until 29 sts. rem. Cast off 3 sts. at beg. of next 4 rows. Cast off.

Front and neck facings

With 3¾ mm. needles and right side facing and with unsequinned yarn, beg. at top of right front hem, pick up and k. 85 (89, 93) sts. along right front edge to shoulder. Beg. p. and inc. 1 st. at beg. of every row, work 7 rows in st. st. Cast off. Beg. at shoulder, work left front edge to match. Picking up 9 (41, 43) sts., finish back neck in the same way.

TO MAKE UP

Do not press. Join shoulder and facing seams. Join shaped edges of facings and hems at lower edge of fronts. Join side and sleeve seams. Set in sleeves. Fold under hems and facings and catch stitch.

Reds

MATERIALS

4 (5) 25 g. balls Hayfield Aspen Mohair in main shade – black (shade 53 009), 2 (3) balls in first contrast shade – raspberry (53 011), 2 (2) balls in second contrast – mulberry (53 001), 4 (5) balls in third contrast – heather (53 015), 3 (4) balls in fourth contrast – burgundy (53 017) and 1 (1) ball in each of 2 further contrasts – blossom pink (53 019) and guard's red (53 018); a pair each 5½ mm. (no. 5) and 5 mm. (no. 6) knitting needles.

TENSION

16 stitches and 18 rows to 10 cm.

MEASUREMENTS

To fit bust 32-34 (36-38) in., 81-86 (91-97) cm.
Length (both sizes) 18½ in., 47 cm.
Sleeve (both sizes) 18½ in., 47 cm.

ABBREVIATIONS

k., knit; p., purl; st(s)., stitch(es); cont., continue; dec., decrease; foll., following; inc(s)., increase(s); patt., pattern; rem., remain(ing); rep., repeat; st. st., stocking stitch; MS, main shade (black); CS, contrast shade (1, raspberry; 2, mulberry; 3, heather; 4, burgundy; 5, blossom pink; 6, guard's red).

NOTE

When changing colours twist yarn to avoid holes (see page 10).

INSTRUCTIONS

Back

With 5 mm. needles and MS, cast on 84 (88) sts. Work in k. 1, p. 1 rib for 10 rows. Change to 5½ mm. needles and work the foll. patt. in st. st. (see page 12):
Row 1: K. 25 (27) in CS1, k. 5 in MS, k. 24 in CS2, k. 5 in MS, k. 25 (27) in CS3.

Row 2: P. 25 (27) in CS3, p. 5 in MS, p. 24 in CS2, p. 5 in MS, p. 25 (27) in CS1. Rep. these 2 rows twelve times more.
Rows 27 to 32: Change to MS and work 6 rows in st. st.
Now rep. these 32 rows, but use CS4, CS5 and CS6 in place of CS1, CS2 and CS3.
** Work rows 1 to 22 once more, using CS3, CS2 and CS1 in that order.

To shape neck Work 31 (33), k. 2 tog., turn: work on these sts. only. Dec. 1 st. at neck edge on next 3 rows, then cast off rem. sts. Slip the centre 18 sts. onto a spare needle to be worked later as Neckband. Rejoin yarn and complete other side of neck to match.

Front

Exactly as Back to **. Work rows 1 to 14 once more, using CS3, CS2 and CS1 in that order.

To shape neck Work 34 (36), k. 2 tog., turn: work on these sts. only. Dec. 1 st. at neck edge on every row until 29 (31) sts. rem., then cont. straight until length matches Back. Cast off.
Slip the centre 12 sts. onto a spare needle to be worked later as Neckband. Rejoin yarn and complete other side of neck to match.

Left sleeve

With 5 mm. needles and MS, cast on 34 (38) sts. Work in k. 1, p. 1 rib for 16 rows, working 6 incs. evenly along last rib row – 40 (44) sts.
Change to 5½ mm. needles and CS3. Work in st. st. but inc. 1 st. at each end of first and every foll. fourth row until there are 74 sts., ending with a p. row.
Change to MS, and still inc. 1 st. at each end of every fourth row, work 8 rows in st. st., then cast off.

Right sleeve

Exactly as Left Sleeve, but use CS4 instead of CS3.
Join right shoulder seam.

Neckband

With 5 mm. needles and right side facing and with MS, pick up and k. 15 sts. along left front neck, k. across the 12 sts. of front neck, pick up and k. 15 sts. along right front neck, 4 sts. along right back neck, k. across the 18 sts. of back neck and pick up and k. 4 sts. along left back neck – 68 sts.
Work in k. 1, p. 1 rib for 11 rows, then cast off ribwise.

TO MAKE UP

Join left shoulder seam and neckband. Fold neckband in half and stitch down on the inside. Set in sleeves. Join sleeve seams and side seams.

Tangled Up In Blue

Simple rectangles of garter stitch make up this easy T-shaped sweater.

Very Easy

MATERIALS

13 (15) 50 g. balls Pingouin Coton Naturel 8 Fils; a pair 6 mm. (no. 4) knitting needles; a crochet hook.

TENSION

15 stitches and 21 rows to 10 cm. over garter stitch.

MEASUREMENTS

To fit bust 32-34 (36-38) in., 81-86 (91-97) cm. very loosely.
Length (both sizes) 28 in., 71 cm.
Sleeve seam (both sizes) 16½ in., 42 cm.

ABBREVIATIONS

k., knit; st(s)., stitch(es); beg., beginning; dec., decrease; g-st., garter stitch; sep., separately; tog., together.

INSTRUCTIONS

Back
Cast on 92 (96) sts. Work in g-st. (see page 12) ** until work measures 69 cm. from beg.

To shape neck K. 31, k. 2 tog., turn: work on these sts. only. Dec. 1 st. at neck edge on the next 3 rows – 29 sts. *Do not cast off.* Cast off centre 26 (30) sts. for neck. Rejoin yarn at neck edge and complete other side to match, reversing shapings.

Front
Work exactly as for Back to ** until work measures 68 cm. from beg.

To shape neck K. 36, cast off centre 20 (24) sts., k. to end. Complete each side sep.
Next row: K. 34, k. 2 tog., turn.
Next row: Cast off 4 sts., k. to end – 31 sts.
Next row: K. 29, k. 2 tog.
Next row: K. 2 tog., k. to end – 29 sts. K. 2 rows. *Do not cast off.* Rejoin yarn and complete other side of neck to match, reversing shapings.

Sleeves
Cast on 68 (72) sts. Work in g-st. until work measures 42 cm. from beg. Cast off loosely.

TO MAKE UP

Graft or cast off shoulder sts. tog. Mark beg. of armhole on back and front 24 cm. down from shoulder. Set in sleeves. Join side and sleeve seams. Neaten neck either by crocheting round neck edge with crochet hook or picking up and casting off with a knitting needle.

Fast and Loose

MATERIALS

7 (8, 8) 50 g. balls Pingouin Pingofrance in black and 5 (6, 6) balls in grey; a pair 5½ mm. (no. 5) knitting needles; a stitch-holder.

TENSION

16 stitches and 18 rows to 10 cm. over stocking stitch, using 5½ mm. needles.

MEASUREMENTS

To fit bust 34 (36, 38) in., 86 (91, 97) cm.
Length 18 (18½, 19) in., 46 (47, 48) cm.
Sleeve seam (all sizes) 15¾ in., 40 cm.

ABBREVIATIONS

k., knit; p., purl; st(s)., stitch(es); beg., beginning; cont., continue; dec., decrease; foll., following; inc., increas(e)(ing); rem., remain(ing); st. st., stocking stitch; tog., together.

NOTE

Yarn is used double throughout.

INSTRUCTIONS

Back

With 5½ mm. needles and two strands of black, cast on 86 (90, 94) sts. K. 10 rows **. Now using one strand of grey and one strand of black, work in st. st. (see page 12) until work measures 43 (44, 45) cm. from beg., ending with a p. row.

To shape neck Next row: K. 32 (34, 36), k. 2 tog., turn: work on these sts. only. Dec. 1 st. at neck edge on next 3 rows. Cast off rem. 30 (32, 34) sts. Slip centre 18 sts. onto a stitch-holder. Rejoin yarn to rem. sts. and complete to match first side.

Front

Work as for Back to **. Now using one strand of grey and one strand of black work in st. st. until Front measures 39 (40, 41) cm. from beg., ending with a p. row.

To shape neck Next row: K. 34 (36, 38), k. 2 tog., turn: work on these sts. only. Dec. 1 st. at neck edge on every row until 30 (32, 34) sts. rem. Cont. in st. st. until work matches Back. Cast off. Slip centre 14 sts. onto a stitch-holder. Rejoin yarn to rem. sts. and complete to match first side.

Sleeves

With 5½ mm. needles and two strands of black, cast on 42 (44, 46) sts. K. 10 rows. Now using one strand of grey and one strand of black work in st. st., inc. 1 st. at each end of next and every foll. fifth row until there are 70 (72, 74) sts. Cast off very loosely.
Join right shoulder seam.

Neckband

With 5½ mm. needles and two strands of black, pick up and k. 4 sts. up right back neck, k. across 18 sts. of back neck, pick up and k. 4 sts. down left back neck, 12 sts. down left front neck, k. across 14 sts. of front neck, and pick up and k. 12 sts. up right front neck — 64 sts.
K. 6 rows. Cast off.

TO MAKE UP

Join left shoulder seam and neckband. Set in sleeves. Join side and sleeve seams. Press all seams.

Flashback

MATERIALS

13 (14, 15) 50 g. balls Pingouin Coton Naturel 8 Fils in fuschia *or* 7 (8, 8) balls Pingouin Mohair 70; a pair each 3¼ mm. (no. 10) and 4 mm. (no. 8) knitting needles; a stitch-holder; a circular 4 mm. (no. 8) needle for working garment in one piece; a circular 3¼ mm. (no. 10) needle for neckband.

TENSION

19 stitches and 28 rows to 10 cm. over pattern, using 4 mm. needles.

MEASUREMENTS

To fit bust 34 (36, 38) in., 86 (91, 97) cm.
Full length (all sizes) 23 in., 58 cm.
Sleeve seam (all sizes) 15 in., 38 cm.

ABBREVIATIONS

k., knit; p., purl; st(s)., stitch(es); alt., alternate; beg., beginning; cont., continue; dec., decrease; foll., following; inc(s)., increase(s); m. 1, make 1 by picking up loop which lies between sts. and k. into back of it; patt., pattern; rem., remaining; rep., repeat; tog., together.

INSTRUCTIONS

Worked in one piece (starting at lower front edge).
With 3¼ mm. needles, cast on 91 (95, 99) sts. Work in k. 1, p. 1 rib as follows:
Row 1: K. 1, * k. 1, p. 1; rep. from * to last 2 sts., k. 2.
Row 2: * K. 1, p. 1; rep. from * to last st., k. 1.
Rep. these 2 rows until work measures 11 cm.
Next row: Rib 12 (10, 7), * m. 1, rib 22 (15, 12); rep. from * three (five, seven) times, m. 1, rib 13 (10, 8) – 95 (101, 107) sts.
Change to 4 mm. needles and work in patt. as follows:
Rows 1 and 3 (wrong side): K.

Rows 2 and 4: P.
Row 5: * K. 5, p. 1; rep. from * to last 5 sts., k. 5.
Row 6: * P. 5, m. 1, k. 1; rep. from * to last 5 sts., p. 5.
Row 7: * K. 5, p. 2; rep. from * to last 5 sts., k. 5.
Row 8: * P. 5, k. 1, m. 1, k. 1; rep. from * to last 5 sts., p. 5.
Row 9: * K. 5, p. 3; rep. from * to last 5 sts., k. 5.
Row 10: * P. 5, k. 2, m. 1, k. 1; rep. from * to last 5 sts., p. 5.
Row 11: * K. 5, p. 4; rep. from * to last 5 sts., k. 5.
Row 12: * P. 5, k. 4 tog.; rep. from * to last 5 sts., p. 5.
Rows 13 to 16: As rows 1 to 4.
Row 17: K. 2, * p. 1, k. 5; rep. from * to last 3 sts., p. 1, k. 2.
Row 18: P. 2, * m. 1, k. 1, p. 5; rep. from * to last 3 sts., m. 1, k. 1, p. 2.
Row 19: K. 2, * p. 2, k. 5; rep. from * to last 4 sts., p. 2, k. 2.
Row 20: P. 2, * k. 1, m. 1, k. 1, p. 5; rep. from * to last 4 sts., k. 1, m. 1, k. 1, p. 2.
Row 21: K. 2, * p. 3, k. 5; rep. from * to last 5 sts., p. 3, k. 2.
Row 22: P. 2, * k. 2, m. 1, k. 1, p. 5; rep. from * to last 5 sts., k. 2, m. 1, k. 1, p. 2.
Row 23: K. 2, * p. 4, k. 5; rep. from * to last 6 sts., p. 4, k. 2.
Row 24: P. 2, * k. 4 tog., p. 5; rep. from * to last 6 sts., k. 4 tog., p. 2.
These 24 rows form patt. Rep. patt. once more, then work rows 1 to 16 again.

To shape sleeves Inc. 1 st. at each end of next 12 rows – 119 (125, 131) sts.
Cast on 24 sts. at beg. of next 4 rows – 215 (221, 227) sts.
Change to 4 mm. circular needle and, working backwards and forwards, cont. straight in patt. until row 14 of fifth patt. rep. has been completed.

To shape neck Patt. 100 (103, 106), turn: leave rem. sts. on a spare needle. Dec. 1 st. at neck edge on next 12 rows. When row 12 of the sixth patt. rep. has been worked, place a marker at each end of row.
Return to sts. left unworked and slip the centre 15 sts. onto a stitch-holder. Rejoin yarn to rem. 100 (103, 106) sts. and complete to match first side. Rejoin yarn to sts. of Left Back and inc. 1 st. at neck edge on every foll. third row until 17 incs. have been worked and length at outer sleeve edge equals length of front sleeve to marked row.

To shape back sleeves Cont. to inc. 1 st. at neck edge as before, but *at the same time*, cast off 24 sts. at sleeve edge on next and foll. alt. row. When 19 incs. have been worked at neck edge, leave sts. on a spare needle. Rejoin yarn to sts. of Right Back and complete to match Left Back.
Next row: Work over all sts. in patt., working 1 inc. at centre – 215 (221, 227) sts.
Complete Back to match Front.

Neckband

With 3¼ mm. circular needle and right side facing, beg. at right back, k. up 42 sts. down right back neck, 1 st. at centre back neck, 42 sts. up left back neck and 26 sts. down left front edge, k. across 15 sts. of front neck, then k. up 26 sts. up right neck edge – 152 sts.
Work in rounds of k. 1, p. 1 rib for 8 rounds. Cast off ribwise.

Cuffs *(two)*

With 3¼ mm. needles and right side facing, k. up 54 sts. along sleeve edge. Work in k. 1, p. 1 rib for 13 rows. Cast off ribwise.

TO MAKE UP

Join side and sleeve seams. Join cuffs.

One Armed Bandit

Adult's sweater

MATERIALS

5 (5) 100 g. balls Jaeger Naturgarn in main shade – natural (shade 254), 2 (2) balls in first contrast shade – kayak (703) and 1 (2) balls in second contrast shade – polar (701); a pair each 5½ mm. (no. 5) and 6½ mm. (no. 3) knitting needles; a circular 5 mm. (no. 6) needle (optional).

TENSION

14 stitches and 18 rows to 10 cm.

MEASUREMENTS

To fit bust 32-34 (36-38) in., 81-86 (91-97) cm.
Length 16½ (17) in., 42 (43) cm.
Sleeve 17 (17½) in., 43 (44) cm.

ABBREVIATIONS

k., knit; p., purl; st(s)., stitch(es); beg., beginning; cont., continue; dec., decrease; foll., following; inc., increase; patt., pattern; rem., remain(ing); rep., repeat; st. st., stocking stitch; tog., together; MS, main shade (natural); A, first contrast shade (kayak); B, second contrast shade (polar).

INSTRUCTIONS

Front

With 5½ mm. needles and MS, cast on 78 (82) sts. Work in k. 2, p. 2 rib for 4 cm., ending with a wrong side row.
Change to 6½ mm. needles and work in st. st. (see page 12), beg. with a k. row, for 22 rows.
Change to A and work in st. st., beg. with a k. row, for 10 rows.
Change to B and work in st. st., beg. with a k. row, for 10 rows.
Change to A and work in st. st., beg. with a k. row, for 10 rows *.
Now change to MS and work in st. st., beg. with a k. row, for 18 rows.

To shape neck K. 28 (30), turn: work on these sts. only. Dec. 1 st. at neck edge

on the next 4 rows. P. 1 row. Cast off. Slip the centre 22 sts. onto a spare needle to be worked later as Roll Collar. Rejoin yarn and complete other side of neck to match.

Back

Exactly as Front to *. Now change to MS and work in st. st., beg. with a k. row, for 24 rows. Cast off 24 (26) sts., slip next 30 sts. onto a spare needle, cast off rem. sts.

One Armed Bandit

Right sleeve *(knitted in MS only)*

With 5½ mm. needles and MS, cast on 46 (50) sts. Work in k. 2, p. 2 rib for 6 cm., ending with a wrong side row.
Now change to 6½ mm. needles and work in st. st. but inc. 1 st. at each end of every foll. sixth row until there are 64 (68) sts. When work measures 43 (44) cm. from beg., cast off.

Left sleeve

With 5½ mm. needles and A, cast on 46 (50) sts. Work in k. 2, p. 2 rib for 6 cm., ending with a wrong side row.
Change to 6½ mm. needles and work as for Left Sleeve, *at the same time* work 60 rows in Stripe Patt. (given below) and for remainder of sleeve cont. in B.

Stripe patt. Work rows 1 to 6 in B.
Work rows 7 to 18 in A.
Rep. rows 1 to 18 twice more, then rows 1 to 6 once again.

Roll collar

Join shoulder seams. With 5 mm. circular needle and right side facing, k. across the 30 sts. of back neck, pick up and k. 6 sts. along left neck edge, k. across the 22 sts. of front neck and pick up and k. 6 sts. along right neck edge – 64 sts.
Work 14 rounds every round k., then cast off. Collar rolls over to show p. side of work. (If you dislike using a circular needle, use an ordinary needle and work to and fro in st. st., then join seam on the k. side of the st. st.)

TO MAKE UP

Press all pieces except rib according to instructions on ball band. Set in sleeves to an armhole length of 21 (22) cm. Join sleeve seams and side seams. Press all seams.

Child's sweater

MATERIALS

3 (3, 4) 100 g. balls Jaeger Naturgarn in main shade – kayak (shade 703) and 1 (1, 1) ball in contrast shade – polar (701); a pair each 6 mm. (no. 4) and 6½ mm. (no. 3) knitting needles.

TENSION

14 stitches and 18 rows to 10 cm.

MEASUREMENTS

To fit chest 24 (26, 28) in., 61 (67, 71) cm.
Length 15¼ (16¾, 18½) in., 38.5 (42.5, 46.5) cm.
Sleeve 12¾ (13½, 16) in., 32 (34, 36) cm.

ABBREVIATIONS

As for Adult's sweater, except MS, main shade (kayak); CS, contrast shade (polar).

INSTRUCTIONS

Front

With 5½ mm. needles and MS, cast on 54 (58, 62) sts. Work in k. 2, p. 2 rib for 4 cm.

Change to 6½ mm. needles and work in st. st. for 16 (22, 28) rows.

Change to CS and work in st. st. for 8 rows.

Change to MS and work in st. st. for 8 rows.

Change to CS and work in st. st. for 8 rows **.

Now change to MS and work in st. st. for 14 rows.

To shape neck K. 17 (19, 21), k. 2 tog., turn: work on these sts. only. Dec. 1 st. at neck edge on every row until 14 (16, 18) sts. rem. Cast off. Slip the centre 16 sts. of row onto a spare needle to be worked later as Roll Collar. Rejoin yarn and complete other side of neck to match.

Back

Exactly as Front to **.

Change to MS and work in st. st. to match Front. Cast off 14 (16, 18) sts. at beg. of next 2 rows. Leave rem. 26 sts. on a spare needle.

Left sleeve *(knitted in MS only)*

With 5½ mm. needles and MS, cast on 30 (32, 34) sts. Work in k. 2, p. 2 rib for 8 rows, but inc. 1 st. at each end of last rib row – 32 (34, 36) sts.

Change to 6½ mm. needles and work in st. st. but inc. 1 st. at each end of the fourth and every foll. eighth row until there are 44 (48, 52) sts. Cast off *loosely*.

Right sleeve *(striped in MS and CS)*

Work as for Left Sleeve, but work in stripes of 4 rows each, starting with CS, then working a stripe in MS, etc. until there are 44 (48, 52) sts. Cast off *loosely*. Join shoulder seams.

Roll collar

With circular 5½ mm. needle and MS and with right side facing, k. across the 24 sts. of back neck, pick up and k. 7 sts. along left neck edge, k. across the 16 sts. of front neck and pick up and k. 7 sts. along right neck edge – 56 sts.

Working in rounds of st. st., cont. until 12 (14, 16) rounds have been completed. Cast off loosely.

TO MAKE UP

Press all pieces except rib according to instructions on ball band. Set in sleeves to an armhole length of 17 (18, 19) cm. Join sleeve seams and side seams. Press all seams.

Easy Rider

MATERIALS

16 (17) 50 g. balls Pingouin Multicolore in noir (shade 11); a pair 6 mm. (no. 4) knitting needles; a circular 5½ mm. (no. 5) needle for neck.

TENSION

13 stitches and 22 rows to 10 cm.

MEASUREMENTS

To fit bust 32-34 (36-38) in., 82-87 (92-97) cm.
Length 24½ (25) in., 62 (63) cm.
Sleeve (both sizes) 17 in., 43 cm.

ABBREVIATIONS

k., knit; p., purl; st(s)., stitch(es); beg., beginning; cont., continue; dec., decrease; foll., following; inc., increase; k. 1b., knit 1 below (k. next st. 1 row below st. on needle, slipping sts. off needle in usual way); patt., pattern; rem., remain; rep., repeat.

> Baggy sweater in brioche rib in brilliantly flecked black, with shaped bottom edges, raglan seams and a loose round neck.

INSTRUCTIONS

Back and front *(alike)*

With 6 mm. needles, cast on 53 (59) sts.
K. 2 rows.
Next row: K. 1, (p. 1, k. 1b.) to last 2 sts., p. 1, k. 1.
Next row: Inc. in first st., (k. 1b., p. 1) to last 2 sts., k. 1b., inc. into last st.
Next row: K. 2, p. 1, (k. 1b., p. 1) to last 2 sts., k. 2.
Next row: Inc. into first st., (p. 1, k. 1b.) to last 2 sts., p. 1, inc. into last st.
Rep. the last 4 rows twice more – 65 (71) sts.
Cont. in patt. thus:
Row 1: K. 1, (p. 1, k. 1b.) to last 2 sts., p. 1, k. 1.
Row 2: K. 1, (k. 1b., p. 1) to last 2 sts., k. 1b., k. 1.
These 2 rows form patt. Cont. in patt. until work measures 43 cm. from beg.

To shape raglans Cast off 4 sts. at beg. of next 2 rows. Dec. 1 st. at each end of next and foll. third row, 1 st. at each end of foll. fourth row, then dec. 1 st. at each end of next and every foll. fifth row until 25 sts. rem. Cast off loosely.

Sleeves

Cast on 25 (26) sts., k. 1 row.
Inc. row: Inc. into each st. to last st., k. 1 – 49 (51) sts.
K. 1 row.
Cont. in patt. as for Back until work measures 43 cm. from beg., ending with a row 2.

To shape top Cast off 4 sts. at beg. of next 2 rows. Dec. 1 st. at each end of next and every foll. third row until 11 sts. rem. Cast off loosely.

TO MAKE UP

Join raglan seams.

Neckband

With circular 5½ mm. needle, pick up and k. 25 sts. along back neck, 11 sts. along left sleeve top, 25 sts. along front neck and 11 sts. along right sleeve top. Work in rounds of k. 1, p. 1 rib until 7 rounds have been completed. Cast off loosely. Join sleeve seams and side seams.

Road Runner

MATERIALS

8 (8, 9) 50 g. balls Pingouin Coton Naturel 8 Fils in yellow; a pair each 3¼ mm. (no. 10) and 4 mm. (no. 8) knitting needles.

TENSION

12 stitches and 13 rows to 5 cm.

MEASUREMENTS

To fit bust 34 (36, 38) in., 86 (91, 97) cm.
Length at underarm 15¾ (16, 16½) in., 40 (41, 42) cm.

ABBREVIATIONS

k., knit; p., purl; st(s)., stitch(es); alt., alternate; beg., beginning; cont., continue; dec., decreas(e)(ing); foll., following; rem., remaining.

INSTRUCTIONS

Back
With 3¼ mm. needles, cast on 102 (110, 118) sts. Work 16 rows in k. 2, p. 2

Long lean vest in double rib has a pick up and cast off edge at neck and armholes.
Very Easy

rib, beg. second row p. 2.
Change to 4 mm. needles *. Cont. in rib until work measures 35 (36, 37) cm. from beg., ending with a wrong side row.

To shape neck Next row: Rib 40 (44, 48), cast off 22 sts., rib 40 (44, 48). Cont. on last set of sts. only. Rib 1 row. Dec. 1 st. at beg. of next and foll. 5 alt. rows.

To shape armhole Cast off 7 (9, 11) sts. at beg. of next row. Still dec. 1 st. at neck edge at beg. of next and foll. 2 alt. rows, *at the same time* cast off 8 (9, 10) sts. at beg. of foll. 2 alt. rows at armhole edge – 8 sts.
Cont. in rib as set until work measures 56 (58, 60) cm. from beg. Cast off ribwise. Rejoin yarn to inner of rem. sts. and work other side to match.

Front
As Back to *. Cont. in rib until work measures 40 (41, 42) cm., ending with a wrong side row.

To shape armhole Cast off 7 (9, 11) sts. at beg. of next 2 rows and 8 (9, 10) sts. at beg. of foll. 4 rows.

To shape neck Next row: Rib 13, cast off 30 sts., rib 13. Cont. on last set of sts. only. Rib 1 row. Dec. 1 st. at beg. of next and foll. 4 alt. rows – 8 sts. Cont. in rib as set until work measures 56 (58, 60) cm. from beg. Cast off ribwise. Rejoin yarn to inner end of rem. sts. and work other side to match.

Neck edging
Join right shoulder seam. With 3¼ mm. needles and right side facing and working 1 st. in from edge, pick up and k. 244 sts. evenly round neck. Cast off knitwise.

Armhole edging
Join left shoulder and neck edging seam. Working 1 st. in from edge and picking up 116 sts., work as Neck Edging. Work right armhole to match.

TO MAKE UP

Press lightly. Taking in 1 st. from each edge, join side seams. Press seams.

Side Kick

Boxy cropped cable sweater with a wide, low neck, knitted in cotton and from side to side, all in one piece.
Easy

MATERIALS

8 (9) 100 g. balls Twilleys Pegasus; a pair each 3¾ mm. (no. 9) and 3¼ mm. (no. 10) knitting needles; a circular 3¼ mm. (no. 10) needle; a cable needle.

TENSION

19 stitches and 26 rows to 10 cm. over stocking stitch.

MEASUREMENTS

To fit bust 32-34 (36-38) in., 81-86 (91-97) cm.
Length 18 (19) in., 46 (48) cm.
Sleeve (both sizes) 15 in., 38 cm.

ABBREVIATIONS

k., knit; p., purl; st(s)., stitch(es); alt., alternate; beg., beginning; cont., continue; C5B, slip next 5 sts. onto cable needle and place at back of work, k. 5, then k. 5 from cable needle; dec., decrease; foll., following; inc(s)., increase(s); patt(s)., pattern(s); rem., remain(ing); rep., repeat; tog., together.

INSTRUCTIONS

Worked in one piece from side to side. Beg. at right sleeve edge with 3¼ mm. needles, cast on 47 (55) sts. Work 15 rows in k. 1, p. 1 rib.
Next row: Work in rib but inc. into every alt. st. to last st., k. 1 – 70 (82) sts.
Change to 3¾ mm. needles and work in cable patt. thus:
Row 1: P. 6 (12), * k. 10, p. 14 *; rep. from * to * to last 16 (22) sts., k. 10, p. 6 (12).
Row 2: K. 6 (12), * p. 10, k. 14 *; rep. from * to * to last 16 (22) sts., k. 10, p. 6 (12).
Rows 3 to 8: As rows 1 and 2.
Row 9: P. 6 (12), * C5B, p. 14 *; rep. from * to * to last 16 (22) sts., C5B, p. 6 (12).
Row 10: As row 2.
Rows 11 to 14: As rows 1 and 2.

These 14 rows form patt. Cont. to work patt., inc. 1 st. at each end of the next eighth row of the second patt. rep. and on every foll. tenth row until there are 80 (86) sts., working the incs. into the patt. Cont. straight until six complete patts. have been worked from beg., then work rows 1 to 6 once more.

To shape sides Inc. 1 st. at each end of the next 4 rows – 88 (100) sts., ending on row 10 of the seventh patt. rep.
Cast on 63 sts. at beg. of next row. Work over these sts. as follows:
P. 6 (12), * k. 10, p. 14 *; rep. from * to * over these 63 sts., then work over main part in patt. Cast on 63 sts. at other end of row, k. 6 (12), * p. 10, k. 14 *; rep. from * to * over these 63 sts., then work to end as patt. row 12. Cont. in cable patt. as set until the ninth patt. has been completed from beg.
Now work rows 1 to 6 once more for 1st size and rows 1 to 12 once more for 2nd size.

To divide for neck With right side facing on patt. row 7 (13), work 107 (113) sts. in patt., turn. Work on these sts. only for Front. Cast off 4 sts., work to end.
Next row: Work in patt. Now dec. 1 st. at neck edge on next and every alt. row until 94 (100) sts. rem. Work 30 rows straight, ending on a patt. row 14 (6). Now inc. 1 st. on the next and every foll. alt. row until there are 103 (109) sts.
Next row: Work in patt. row 4 (10).
Next row: Work in patt.
Next row: Cast on 4 sts., work in patt. to end – 107 (113) sts.
Break yarn and leave sts. on a spare needle. Rejoin yarn to rem. sts. and work back neck. Cast off 4 sts., patt. to end – 103 (109) sts.
Next row: Work in patt.
Now dec. 1 st. at neck edge on next 4 rows – 99 (105) sts.

Work straight in patt. until the fourteenth patt. from beg. has been completed. Now work rows 1 and 2 once more for 1st size and rows 1 to 8 once more for 2nd size.
Inc. 1 st. at neck edge on next 4 rows – 103 (109) sts., ending with a patt. row 6 (12). Cast on 4 sts. at neck edge.

To join front and back Return to Front, rejoin yarn and working a patt. row 7 (13), work over the 107 (113) sts. of Front and the 107 (113) sts. of Back – 214 (226) sts.
Cont. in patt. until 3 patts. and 0 (6) rows have been completed from the end of neck shaping, ending with a row 6 of eighteenth patt. for 1st size and row 4 of nineteenth patt. for 2nd size.

To shape sides Cast off 63 sts. at beg. of next 2 rows – 88 (100) sts.
Now dec. 1 st. at each end of the next 4 rows – 80 (92) sts.

To shape left sleeve Work 28 rows straight in cable patt., then dec. 1 st. at each end of next and every foll. tenth row until 70 (82) sts. rem. Now work 21 rows straight in patt.
Dec. row: K. 1, k. 2 tog. to last st., k. 1 – 47 (55) sts.
Change to 3¼ mm. needles and work 15 rows in k. 1, p. 1 rib. Cast off ribwise.

Neckband

With 3¼ mm. circular needle and right side facing, beg. at back right shoulder, pick up and k. 56 sts. evenly along back neck edge, then 54 sts. evenly along front neck edge. Work 8 rounds in k. 1, p. 1 rib. Cast off ribwise.

Lower welt (back and front alike)

With 3¼ mm. needles and right side facing, pick up and k. 91 (101) sts. along bottom edge. Work 9 rows in k. 1, p. 1 rib. Cast off ribwise.

TO MAKE UP

Join side and sleeve seams. Press all seams lightly on the wrong side with a warm iron over a damp cloth.

Subtle Hint

Fine cotton cardigan with an all-over chevron pattern has ribbed, padded shoulders, garter stitch front bands and tiny pearl buttons.

MATERIALS

12 (13) 50 g. balls Twilleys Stalite in white (shade 78); a pair each 3 mm. (no. 11) and 3¼ mm. (no. 10) knitting needles; six buttons; two shoulder pads.

TENSION

26 stitches and 34 rows to 10 cm., using 3¼ mm. needles.

MEASUREMENTS

To fit bust 32-34 (36-38) in., 81-86 (91-97) cm.
Length 22 (22½) in., 56 (57) cm.
Sleeve (both sizes) 17 in., 43 cm.

ABBREVIATIONS

k., knit; p., purl; st(s)., stitch(es); alt., alternate; beg., beginning; cont., continue; dec., decrease; foll., following; g-st., garter stitch; inc., increase; patt., pattern; rem., remain(ing).

INSTRUCTIONS

Back

With 3 mm. needles, cast on 114 (130) sts. Work in k. 2, p. 2 rib for 7 cm., ending with a right side row.
Inc. row: Inc. into every fourth st., rib 2 – 142 (162) sts.
Change to 3¼ mm. needles and work the foll. patt. (worked over multiples of 10 sts., with a selvedge st. at each end):
Row 1: P.
Row 2: K.
Row 3: K. 1, (k. 1, p. 9) to last st., p. 1.
Row 4 and alt. rows: K. the k. sts. and p. the p. sts. as they face you.
Row 5: K. 1, (k. 2, p. 7, k. 1) to last st., k. 1.
Row 7: K. 1, (k. 3, p. 5, k. 2) to last st., k. 1.
Row 9: K. 1, (k. 4, p. 3, k. 3) to last st., k. 1.
Row 11: K. 1, (p. 1, k. 4) to last st., k. 1.

Row 13: K. 1, (p. 2, k. 7, p. 1) to last st., k. 1.
Row 15: K. 1, (p. 3, k. 5, p. 2) to last st., k. 1.
Row 17: K. 1, (p. 4, k. 3, p. 3) to last st., k. 1.
Row 19: K. 1, (k. 1, p. 4) to last st., k. 1.
Row 20: P. 1, (p. 1, k. 9) to last st., p. 1.
When rows 1 to 20 have been completed, work the patt. from row 5 only thereafter. These 16 rows form patt. Cont. in patt. until work measures 36 (37) cm. from beg.

To shape armholes Cast off 6 sts. at beg. of next 2 rows. Now dec. 1 st. at each end of every alt. row four times in all – 122 (142) sts.
When patt. has been worked twice from beg. of armhole shaping, work in k. 2, p. 2 rib until work measures 20 (20) cm. from beg. of armhole shaping. Cast off.

Left front

With 3 mm. needles, cast on 62 (70) sts. Work in k. 2, p. 2 rib for 7 cm., ending with a right side row.
Inc. row: Rib 10 (6), inc. into next and every foll. fifth st. to last 2 (2) sts., rib 2 (2) – 72 (82) sts.
Work as Back to armhole shaping.

To shape armhole At armhole edge, cast off 6 sts., then dec. 1 st. on foll. 4 alt. rows – 62 (72) sts.
When patt. has been worked twice from beg. of armhole shaping, work in k. 2, p. 2 rib for 7 cm., ending at neck edge.

To shape neck Cast off 20 sts., rib to end – 42 (52) sts.
Next row: Rib to end.
Next row: Cast off 12 sts., rib to end – 30 (40) sts.
Now dec. 1 st. at same edge on next 2 rows. Cont. in rib until length from beg.

of armhole matches that of Back. Cast off.

Right front

As Left Front, reversing all shapings.

Sleeves

With 3 mm. needles, cast on 70 (78) sts. Work in k. 2, p. 2 rib for 7 cm., ending with a right side row.
Inc. row: Inc. into every third st. to last 4 (6) sts., rib 4 (6) – 92 (102) sts.
Change to 3¼ mm. needles and work in patt. as set for Back until work measures 43 cm. from beg.

To shape armholes Cast off 6 sts. at beg. of next 2 rows – 80 (90) sts.
Now dec. 1 st. at each end of every alt. row until 34 sts. rem. Cast off 5 sts. at beg. of next 4 rows. Cast off rem. sts.

Front bands

With 3 mm. needles, cast on 10 sts. Work 8 rows in g-st. (see page 12).
Buttonhole row: K. 4, cast off 2 sts., k. to end.
Next row: K. 4, cast on 2 sts., k. to end. Work 5 more buttonholes, each spaced 32 rows apart. Work 8 more rows, then cast off. Work a band of similar length for Left Front, but without buttonholes.

TO MAKE UP

Join shoulder seams, matching the rib. Set in sleeves. Join sleeve seams and side seams. Stitch on front bands. Sew on buttons. Sew in shoulder pads.

Neckbands

With 3 mm. needles and right side facing, beg. at right front and k. across the 10 sts. of right front band, pick up and k. 28 sts. along right front edge, 52 sts. along back neck, and 28 sts. along left neck edge, then k. across the 10 sts. of left front band. K. 7 rows. Cast off.

Beau Jest

MATERIALS

8 (9, 10) 50 g. balls Pingouin Confort in black and 1 (1, 1) ball in each of 2 contrast shades (red and white); a pair each 3¼ mm. (no. 10) and 3¾ mm. (no. 9) knitting needles; a circular 3¼ mm. (no. 10) needle.

TENSION

23 stitches and 31 rows to 10 cm. over stocking stitch, using 3¾ mm. needles.

MEASUREMENTS

To fit bust 34 (36, 38) in., 86 (91, 97) cm.

Schiaparelli-inspired bow sweater in bold black, red and white has padded shoulders and a square neckline.

Length 22½ (22¾, 23¼) in., 57 (58, 59) cm.
Sleeve (all sizes) 17 in., 43 cm.

ABBREVIATIONS

k., knit; p., purl; st(s)., stitch(es); alt., alternate; beg., beginning; cont., continue; dec., decrease; foll., following; inc(s)., increase(s); rem., remain(ing); sep., separately; st. st., stocking stitch; MS, main shade (black); CS1, first contrast shade (white); CS2, second contrast shade (red).

NOTE

See page 10 for information on reading a chart.

INSTRUCTIONS

Back
With 3¼ mm. needles and MS, cast on 116 (122, 128) sts. Work in k. 1, p. 1 rib for 5 cm.
Change to 3¾ mm. needles **.
Cont. in st. st. (see page 12) until work measures 38 cm. from beg., ending with a p. row.

To shape armholes Cast off 7 sts. at beg. of next 2 rows and 3 sts. at beg. of foll. 2 rows. Now dec. 1 st. at each end of foll. 3 alt. rows – 90 (96, 102) sts.
Cont. straight in st. st. until armhole measures 17 (18, 19) cm., ending with a p. row.

To shape neck K. 28 (31, 34), slip centre 34 sts. onto a spare needle to be worked later as Neckband, k. to end. Finish each side sep. Dec. 1 st. at neck edge on every row until 22 (25, 28) sts. rem. Cast off. Rejoin yarn and complete other side of neck to match.

Front
Work as for Back to **. Cont. in st. st. until work measures 26 cm. from beg., ending with a p. row.
Now work the fair isle bow from Chart as follows:
Row 1: K. 35 (38, 41), work across row 1 of Chart, k. 35 (38, 41). Cont. thus in st. st. until work measures same as Back to armhole, ending with a p. row.

To shape armholes Keeping fair isle correct, cast off 7 sts. at beg. of next 2 rows and 3 sts. at beg. of foll. 2 rows.

KEY
Pingouin Confort

□ main shade (black)   ✕ white   ○ red

Read odd-numbered (right side) rows from right to left, and even-numbered (wrong side) rows from left to right.

Beau Jest

33) sts. along front right neck edge, 8 sts. along back right neck edge, then work over the 34 sts. of back neck in k. 1, p. 1 rib – 156 (160, 164) sts.

Work 8 rounds in k. 1, p. 1 rib but dec. 1 st. on every alt. row at each side of the 2 marked sts. Cast off ribwise.

TO MAKE UP

Set in sleeves. Join sleeve seams and side seams.

Now dec. 1 st. at each end of foll. 3 alt. rows – 90 (96, 102) sts.

Cont. working from Chart until row 56 has been completed. Work 2 more rows in st. st., thus ending with a p. row.

To shape neck K. 22 (25, 28), turn: work on these sts. only. Work straight until length matches Back. Cast off. Slip centre 46 sts. onto a spare needle to be worked later as Neckband. Rejoin yarn to rem. sts. and complete other side of neck to match.

Sleeves

With 3¼ mm. needles and MS, cast on 52 (56, 60) sts. Work in k. 1, p. 1 rib for 7 cm., working 18 incs. evenly along last rib row – 70 (74, 78) sts.

Change to 3¾ mm. needles and cont. in st. st. but inc. 1 st. at each end of every foll. tenth row until there are 82 (86, 90) sts. and work measures 43 cm. from beg., ending with a p. row.

To shape top Cast off 7 sts. at beg. of next 2 rows, then dec. 1 st. at each end of every alt. row until 26 sts. rem. Cast off 5 sts. at beg. of next 2 rows then cast off rem. sts.

Neckband

Join shoulder seams. With 3¼ mm. circular needle and right side facing and with MS, pick up and k. 8 sts. along back left neck edge, 29 (31, 33) sts. along left front neck edge, 1 st. in left hand corner (marking this st. with a coloured thread), then work over the 46 sts. of front neck in k. 1, p. 1 rib, pick up and k. 1 st. in right hand corner (marking this st. with a coloured thread), pick up and k. 29 (31,

Mosaic

MATERIALS

Knitted in Maxwell Cartlidge 'Silks' (pure silk), available by mail order only from Maxwell Cartlidge, PO Box 33, Colchester, Essex, CO1 1EQ.
3 50 g. balls Maxwell Cartlidge silk in main shade – cream (shade S5L), 2 50 m. hanks in each of 3 contrast shades – bronze (S5B), rosedust (S5J) and damask (S5U), and 1 50 g. ball in each of 4 further contrast shades – russett (S5T), camel (S5R), mustard (S5P) and mink (S5H); a pair each 2¼ mm. (no. 13) and 3 mm. (no. 11) knitting needles; a stitch-holder; three small buttons.

TENSION

32 stitches and 32 rows to 10 cm.

MEASUREMENTS

One size only.
To fit bust 32-36 in., 82-92 cm. (Actual size 38½ in., 98 cm.)
Length 22 in., 56 cm.
Sleeve 16½ in., 42 cm.

ABBREVIATIONS

k., knit; p., purl; st(s)., stitch(es); alt., alternate; beg., beginning; cont., continue; dec., decrease; foll., following; inc(s)., increase(s); patt., pattern; rem., remain(ing); sep., separately; st. st., stocking stitch; tog., together; y.r.n., yarn round needle; MS, main shade (cream); CS, contrast shade (1, bronze; 2, russett; 3, camel; 4, mustard; 5, rosedust; 6, damask; 7, mink).

NOTE

See pages 11 and 10 for information on knitting with silk and reading a chart.

INSTRUCTIONS

Back

With 2¼ mm. needles and MS, cast on

Classic pure silk fair isle sweater using seven different contrast shades has three tiny mother-of-pearl buttons fastening the neck. The fair isle pattern is easy to work as you never use more than two colours in any row.
Easy Fair Isle

145 sts. Work in k. 1, p. 1 rib (beg. alt. rows p. 1) for 6 cm., working 9 incs. evenly along last rib row – 154 sts.
Change to 3 mm. needles and work 4 rows in st. st. (see page 12).
Now work fair isle from Chart (working 1 extra k. st. at each end of every row for selvedge), working rows 1 to 72 once, then working rows 1 to 20 once more. Cont. to work fair isle from Chart while shaping armholes as follows:

To shape armholes Cast off 8 sts. at beg. of next 2 rows. ** Dec. 1 st. at each end of every alt. row until 114 sts. rem. Cont. straight in fair isle until row 72 of second patt. rep. has been completed. Now work rows 1 to 4 of Chart then, using MS only, cont. as follows:

To shape neck and shoulders K. 38, cast off 38 sts., k. to end. Finish each side sep.
Cast off 11 sts. at shoulder edge on next and foll. alt. row, and *at the same time* dec. 1 st. at neck edge on the foll. 4 rows. Cast off rem. 12 sts. Rejoin yarn and complete other side of neck to match.

Front

Work as for Back to **.

To divide for neck opening Next row: K. 64, turn: work on these sts. only. Dec. 1 st. at armhole edge on next and every foll. alt. row until 52 sts. rem., thus ending row 46 of second patt. Work 1 row, thus ending at front edge.

To shape neck Cast off 4 sts. at beg. of next and foll. 3 alt. rows. Dec. 1 st. at neck edge on every row until 34 sts. rem. Work straight until patt. matches Back to beg. of shoulder shaping, ending at armhole edge.

To shape shoulder Cast off 11 sts. at beg. of next and foll. alt. row. Work 1

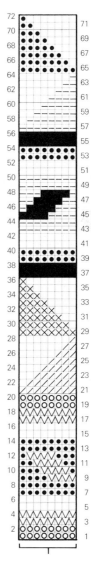

Multiples of 8 sts., with 1 selvedge st. at each end of every row.
Read odd-numbered (k.) rows from right to left, and even-numbered (p.) rows from left to right.

Mosaic

row. Cast off rem. 12 sts.
Now cast off middle 10 sts. and work other side of neck to match.

Sleeves

With 2¼ mm. needles and MS, cast on 57 sts. Work in k. 1, p. 1 rib (beg. alt. rows p. 1) for 7 cm., working 23 incs. evenly along last rib row – 80 sts.
Change to 3 mm. needles. Now work fair isle from Chart, working rows 57 to 72 once. Now work from beg. of Chart, working rows 1 to 72 once, then rows 1 to 20 once more, but at the same time inc. 1 st. at each end of every foll. eighth row until there are 102 sts. When row 20 has been completed, cont. to work from Chart while shaping top as follows:

To shape top Cast off 8 sts. at beg. of next 2 rows. Dec. 1 st. at each end of every foll. alt. row until 64 sts. rem. Work straight for 8 rows. Dec. 1 st. at each end of every alt. row until 50 sts. rem.
Next row: Cast off, working k. 2 tog. all along row.

Button band

* With 2¼ mm. needles and MS, cast on 15 sts.
Row 1: K. 2, (p. 1, k. 1) to last st., k. 1.
Row 2: K. 1, (p. 1, k. 1) to end *.
Rep. these 2 rows thirteen times more.
Leave sts. on a stitch-holder.

Buttonhole band

Work as for Button Band from * to *.
Rep. rows 1 and 2 four times more.
Buttonhole row: Rib 6, p. 2 tog., y.r.n., rib 7.
Rib 9 rows, then work buttonhole row again. Rib 8 rows.

Neckband

Join shoulder seams.
Onto same needle as buttonhole band, pick up and k. 47 sts. along right side of neck, 59 sts. along back neck, 47 sts. along left side of neck then rib 15 sts. of button band – 183 sts. Making last buttonhole as set at beg. of second row, rib 7 rows. Cast off ribwise.

TO MAKE UP

Press work (excluding rib) on the reverse side with warm iron and a damp cloth. Sew one edge of each band to sides of front opening. Overlap bands and sew ends to centre cast off stitches. Sew on buttons. Set in sleeves. Join side seams and sleeve seams. Press all seams.

Hussy

Sexy angora cardigan, designed in two halves, is knitted in double rib and buttons up the front and down the back, to be worn as revealingly as you wish.

Easy

MATERIALS

12 (13, 14) 20 g. balls Jaeger Angora Spun in terracotta (shade 559); a pair 3¼ mm. (no. 10) knitting needles; 28 small buttons.

TENSION

36 stitches and 34 rows to 10 cm. over rib.

MEASUREMENTS

To fit bust 34 (36, 38) in., 86 (91, 97) cm.
Length 20½ (21, 21½) in., 52 (53, 54) cm.
Sleeve (all sizes) 16 in., 41 cm.

ABBREVIATIONS

k., knit; p., purl; st(s)., stitch(es); alt., alternate; beg., beginning; cont., continue; foll., following; rep., repeat.

INSTRUCTIONS

Garment is worked in two halves.

Right half (front)

Cast on 82 (86, 90) sts. and work in k. 2, p. 2 rib as follows:
Row 1: * K. 2, p. 2; rep. from * to last 2 sts., k. 2.
Row 2: * P. 2, k. 2; rep. from * to last 2 sts., p. 2.
Rep. rows 1 and 2 three times more.
Next row (buttonhole row): K. 2, cast off 2 sts., rib to end.
Next row: Rib to last 2 sts., cast on 2 sts., p. 2.
Cont. working in k. 2, p. 2 rib, making buttonholes each spaced 8 rows apart until 12 buttonholes have been worked. Work 5 more rows in rib.

To shape sleeve Cont. working a further 2 buttonholes, spaced 8 rows apart as before, and *at the same time* cast on 10 sts. at sleeve edge on next and foll.

9 alt. rows, then 20 sts. on foll. 2 alt. rows – 222 (226, 230) sts.
Work straight in rib until sleeve edge measures 22 (24, 26) cm., ending at sleeve edge **.
Cast off 20 sts. at beg. of next and foll. alt. row, then 10 sts. on foll. 10 alt. rows – 82 (86, 90) sts.
Work straight to match Front, omitting buttonholes. Cast off ribwise.

Left half (front)

Work as for Right Half to **, omitting buttonholes and reversing sleeve shapings.

Cast off 20 sts. at beg. of next and foll. alt. row, then 10 sts. at beg. of foll. 2 alt. rows.
Work 1 row.
Next row: Cast off 10 sts., rib to last 4 sts., cast off 2 sts., rib 2.
Next row: Rib 2, cast on 2 sts., rib to end.
Cast off 10 sts. at beg. of next and foll. 6 alt. rows and *at the same time* working buttonholes 8 rows apart – 82 (86, 90) sts.
Cont. straight in rib, working buttonholes spaced 8 rows apart until there are 14 buttonholes.
Rib 8 rows. Cast off ribwise.

TO MAKE UP

Join side and sleeve seams. Sew on buttons.

Carte Blanche

MATERIALS

8 (9) 100 g. balls Twilleys Pegasus; a pair each 3¼ mm. (no. 10) and 3¾ mm. (no. 9) knitting needles; a cable needle.

TENSION

21 stitches and 28 rows to 10 cm. over stocking stitch.

MEASUREMENTS

To fit bust 32-34 (36-38) in., 81-86 (91-97) cm.
Length 22 (22½) in., 56 (57) cm.
Sleeve seam (both sizes) 16 in., 41 cm.

ABBREVIATIONS

k., knit; p., purl; st(s)., stitch(es); alt., alternate; beg., beginning; cont., continue; C3B, slip next st. onto cable needle and hold at back of work, k. 3, then p. 1 from cable needle; C3F, slip next 3 sts. onto cable needle and hold at front of work, p. 1, then k. 3 from cable needle; dec., decrease; foll., following; inc., increase; MB, make bobble by working (k. 1, p. 1, k. 1, p. 1) all into next st., then lifting 1st, 2nd and 3rd sts. over 4th st.; patt., pattern; rem., remain; rep., repeat; st. st., stocking stitch.

INSTRUCTIONS

Back

With 3¼ mm. needles, cast on 106 (110) sts. Work 9 rows in k. 2, p. 2 rib.
Next row: Inc. into first st., rib 51 (53), inc. into next 3 sts., rib to last st., inc. into last st. – 111 (115) sts.
Change to 3¾ mm. needles and work the foll. patt.:
Row 1 (wrong side): P. 46 (48), k. 6, p. 3, k. 1, p. 3, k. 6, p. 46 (48).
Row 2: K. 46 (48), p. 6, slip the next 4 sts. onto cable needle and hold at back of work, k. 3 from left hand needle, slip the p. 1 from cable needle onto left hand

White cotton top with little shaping, has a diamond and Aran pattern down the centre.

needle and p. 1, then k. 3 from cable needle, p. 6, k. 46 (48).
Row 3: As row 1.
Row 4: K. 46 (48), p. 5, C3B, k. 1, C3F, p. 5, k. 46 (48).
Row 5 and alt. rows: K. the k. sts. and p. the p. sts.
Row 6: K. 46 (48), p. 4, C3B, k. 1, p. 1, k. 1, C3F, p. 4, k. 46 (48).
Row 8: K. 46 (48), p. 3, C3B, (k. 1, p. 1) twice, k. 1, C3F, p. 3, k. 46 (48).
Row 10: K. 46 (48), p. 2, C3B, (k. 1, p. 1) three times, k. 1, C3F, p. 2, k. 46 (48).
Row 12: K. 46 (48), p. 1, C3B, (k. 1, p. 1) four times, k. 1, C3F, p. 1, k. 46 (48).
Row 14: K. 46 (48), p. 1, C3F, (p. 1, k. 1) four times, p. 1, C3B, p. 1, k. 46 (48).
Row 16: K. 46 (48), p. 2, C3F, (p. 1, k. 1) three times, p. 1, C3B, p. 2, k. 46 (48).
Row 18: K. 46 (48), p. 3, C3F, (p. 1, k. 1) twice, p. 1, C3B, p. 3, k. 46 (48).
Row 20: K. 46 (48), p. 4, C3F, p. 1, k. 1, p. 1, C3B, p. 4, k. 46 (48).
Row 22: K. 46 (48), p. 5, C3F, p. 1, C3B, p. 5, k. 46 (48).
Row 24: As row 2.
Row 26: K. 46 (48), p. 5, C3B, p. 1, C3F, p. 5, k. 46 (48).
Row 28: K. 46 (48), p. 4, C3B, p. 1, MB, p. 1, C3F, p. 4, k. 46 (48).
Row 30: K. 46 (48), p. 4, k. 3, p. 2, MB, p. 2, k. 3, p. 4, k. 46 (48).
Row 32: K. 46 (48), p. 4, C3F, p. 1, MB, p. 1, C3B, p. 4, k. 46 (48).
Row 34: As row 22 **.
These 34 rows form patt. Rep. patt. four times in all.

To shape neck K. 40 (42), slip centre 31 sts. onto a spare needle to be worked later as Neckband, k. 40 (42). Work on last set of sts. only. Dec. 1 st. at neck edge on every row until 35 (37) sts. rem. Cast off. Rejoin yarn and complete other side of neck to match.

Front

As Back to **. Rep. patt. three times in all, then work rows 1 to 30 once more.

To shape neck K. 43 (45), slip centre 25 sts. onto a spare needle to be worked later as Neckband, k. 43 (45). Work on last set of sts. only. Dec. 1 st. at neck edge on every row until 35 (37) sts. rem. Work 2 rows then cast off. Rejoin yarn and complete other side of neck to match.

Sleeves

With 3¾ mm. needles, cast on 84 (90) sts. K. 8 rows. Now cont. in st. st. (see page 12) until work measures 36 cm. from beg. Cast off.

Neckband

Join right shoulder seam. With 3¼ mm. needles and right side facing, beg. at left neck edge, pick up and k. 14 (16) sts. along left neck edge, k. the 25 sts. of front neck, pick up and k. 14 (16) sts. along right neck edge, 7 (9) sts. along right back neck edge, k. the 31 sts. of back neck and pick up and k. 7 (9) sts. along left back neck edge – 98 (106) sts. Work 7 rows in k. 2, p. 2 rib, then cast off ribwise.

TO MAKE UP

Join left shoulder and neckband seams. Set in sleeves. Join sleeve seams and side seams. Press all seams.

Angel Delight

MATERIALS

3 (3, 4) 50 g. balls Twilleys Capricorn Soft Brushed D.K. in main shade, 2 (2, 2) balls in each of 2 contrast shades and 1 (2, 2) balls in each of 3 further contrast shades; a pair each 3¼ mm. (no. 10) and 4 mm. (no. 8) knitting needles; a circular 3¼ mm. (no. 10) needle.

TENSION

23 stitches and 28 rows to 10 cm. over pattern, using 4 mm. needles.

MEASUREMENTS

To fit bust 32-34 (36-38, 40-42) in., 81-86 (91-97, 102-107) cm.
Length from shoulder 23 (23½, 24) in., 59 (60, 61) cm.
Sleeve (all sizes) 15½ in., 40 cm.

ABBREVIATIONS

k., knit; p., purl; st(s)., stitch(es); alt., alternate; beg., beginning; cont., continue; dec., decrease; foll., following; inc., increase; m. 1, make one by picking up loop lying between needles and working into the back of it; patt., pattern; p.s.s.o., pass slip stitch over; rem., remain(ing); rep., repeat; sl., slip; tog., together; A, main shade; B, C, D, E, F, contrast shades.

INSTRUCTIONS

Front

* With 3¼ mm. needles and A, cast on 98 (110, 122) sts.
Rib row 1 (right side): K. 2, (p. 2, k. 2) to end.
Rib row 2: P. 2, (k. 2, p. 2) to end.
Rep. these 2 rows seven times more, then rib row 1 once more.
Inc. row: Rib 7, (m. 1, rib 12) seven (eight, nine) times, m. 1, rib to end – 106 (119, 132) sts.
Change to 4 mm. needles. Joining in and cutting off colours as required, work in patt. as follows:

Pastel chevron striped sweater with garter stitch ridges and a small crossover collar.

Rows 1 and 2: K. with A.
Row 3: With B, (k. 2, m. 1, k. 4, sl. 1, k. 2 tog., p.s.s.o., k. 4, m. 1) to last 2 sts., k. 2.
Row 4: P. with B.
Rows 5 to 12: Rep. rows 3 and 4 four times more.
Rows 13 to 24: As rows 1 to 12 but using C instead of B.
Rows 25 to 36: As rows 1 to 12 but using D instead of B.
Rows 37 to 48: As rows 1 to 12 but using E instead of B.
Rows 49 to 60: As rows 1 to 12 but using F instead of B.
These 60 rows form patt. Cont. in patt. until Front measures 40 cm. from cast on edge, ending with a wrong side row.

To shape armholes Keeping patt. correct, cast off 6 sts. at beg. of next 2 rows and 4 sts. at beg. of foll. 2 rows. Dec. 1 st. at each end of every foll. alt. row until 80 (93, 106) sts. rem. *. Work straight until Front measures 52 (53, 54) cm. from cast on edge, ending with a wrong side row.

To divide for neck Patt. to within last 50 (58, 66) sts., turn and leave rem. sts. on a spare needle. Work on first set of sts. as follows:
** Dec. 1 st. at neck edge on next 8 (9, 10) rows – 22 (26, 30) sts.
Work straight until Front measures 59 (60, 61) cm. from cast on edge, ending at armhole edge. Cast off **.
With right side facing, join yarn to inner end of sts. on spare needle, cast off 20 (23, 26) sts., patt. to end of row. Complete as given for the first side from ** to **.

Back

Work as given for Front from * to *.
Work straight until Back measures same as Front to shoulders, ending with a wrong side row. Cast off.

Sleeves

With 3¼ mm. needles and A, cast on 58 (66, 66) sts. Work 17 rows in rib as Front welt.
Inc. row: Rib 8 (7, 7), (m. 1, rib 2) twenty-one (twenty-six, twenty-six) times, m.1, rib to end – 80 (93, 93) sts.
Change to 4 mm. needles and work in patt. as Front until Sleeves measure 40 cm. from cast on edge, ending same patt. row as Front and Back.

To shape top Keeping patt. correct, cast off 6 sts. at beg. of next 2 rows and 4 sts. at beg. of foll. 2 rows. Dec. 1 st. at each end of every foll. alt. row until 30 (41, 37) sts. rem. Cast off 4 (4, 3) sts. at beg. of next 2 (4, 4) rows. Cast off.

Neckband

Join shoulder seams. With 3¼ mm. circular needle and right side facing, join in A and beg. at centre of front neck, k. 32 (34, 36) sts. up right front neck, 46 (50, 54) sts. from back neck and 32 (34, 36) sts. from left front neck to centre front – 110 (118, 126) sts.
Working backwards and forwards in rows and beg. rib row 2, work as given for Front welt for 1 row. Keeping rib correct, inc. 1 st. at each end of next 9 rows. Cast off.

TO MAKE UP

Do not press. Join sleeves to main part, matching centre of each sleeve top with shoulder seam, then join side and sleeve seams. Cross ends of neckband right over left and stitch on wrong side.

Bel-Ami

MATERIALS

15 (16) 50 g. balls Pingouin Coton Naturel 8 Fils in pale pink; a pair each 3¼ mm. (no. 10) and 4 mm. (no. 8) knitting needles; a cable needle; a 4 mm. crochet hook; one button.

TENSION

21 stitches and 26 rows to 10 cm. over stocking stitch, using 4 mm. needles.

MEASUREMENTS

To fit bust 32-34 (36-38) in., 82-87 (92-97) cm.
Length 23¼ (23½) in., 59 (60) cm.
Sleeve seam (both sizes) 17 in., 43 cm.

ABBREVIATIONS

k., knit; p., purl; st(s)., stitch(es); alt., alternate; beg., beginning; cont., continue; C10F, slip next 5 sts. onto cable needle and place at front of work, k. 5, then k. 5 from cable needle; dec(s)., decrease(s); foll., following; inc(s)., increase(s); patt(s)., pattern(s); p.s.s.o., pass slip stitch over; rem., remain(ing); rep., repeat; sep., separately; sl., slip; y.r.n., yarn round needle.

NOTE

This pattern loses stitches on 3rd, 7th and 11th pattern rows but returns to normal number on 4th, 8th and 12th rows. When counting stitches or shaping, make allowance for this.

INSTRUCTIONS

Back

With 3¼ mm. needles, cast on 102 (110) sts. Work in k. 2, p. 2 rib for 14 rows, beg. and ending alt. rows p. 2.
Inc. row: Rib 4 (5), * inc. in next st., rib 2;

Bel-Ami

rep. from * to last 2 (3) sts., rib to end – 134 (144) sts.
Change to 4 mm. needles and work the foll. patt.:
Row 1: P. 2, (k. 3, p. 2) once (twice), * k. 10, p. 2, (k. 3, p. 2) twice *; rep. from * to * to last 17 (22) sts., k. 10, p. 2, (k. 3, p. 2) once (twice).
Row 2: K. 2, (p. 3, k. 2) once (twice), * p. 10, k. 2, (p. 3, k. 2) twice *; rep. from * to * to last 17 (22) sts., p. 10, k. 2, (p. 3, k. 2) once (twice).
Row 3: P. 2, (sl. 1, k. 2, p.s.s.o. the 2 sts., p. 2) once (twice), * k. 10, p. 2, (sl. 1, k. 2, p.s.s.o. the 2 sts., p. 2) twice *; rep. from * to * to last 17 (22) sts., k. 10, p. 2, (sl. 1, k. 2, p.s.s.o. the 2 sts., p. 2) once (twice).
Row 4: K. 2, (p. 1, y.r.n., p. 1, k. 2) once (twice), * p. 10, k. 2, (p. 1, y.r.n., p. 1, k. 2) twice *; rep. from * to * last 16 (20) sts., p. 10, k. 2, (p. 1, y.r.n., p. 1, k. 2) once (twice).
Row 5: As row 1.
Row 6: As row 2.
Row 7: P. 2, (sl. 1, k. 2, p.s.s.o. the 2 sts., p. 2) once (twice), * C10F, p. 2, (sl. 1, k. 2, p.s.s.o. the 2 sts., p. 2) twice *; rep. from * to * to last 17 (22) sts., C10F, p. 2, (sl. 1, k. 2, p.s.s.o. the 2 sts., p. 2) once (twice).
Row 8: As row 4.
Row 9: As row 1.
Row 10: As row 2.
Row 11: As row 3.
Row 12: As row 4.
These 12 rows form patt. Cont. in patt. until work measures approx. 39 cm. from beg. (i.e. when patt. has been worked seven times in all, and rows 1 to 8 have been worked once more).

To shape armholes Cast off 7 sts. at beg. of next 2 rows and 4 sts. at beg. of foll. 2 rows. Dec. 1 st. at each end of foll. 4 alt. rows – 104 (114) sts. **. (Beg. and end of right side rows will now be k. 2 (7) sts.)
Cont. until work measures 19 (20) cm. from beg. of armhole shaping.

To shape neck Work 31 (36), cast off middle 42 sts., work to end. Finish each side sep. Dec. 1 st. at neck edge on every row until 29 (34) sts. rem. Cast off.

Rejoin yarn and complete other side to match.

Front
Exactly as Back to **.

To shape neck Work 31 (36), lift loop between sts. and p. into the back of it – 32 (37) sts.
Work patt. over these sts. only. When 10 patts. have been completed from beg., work rows 1 to 8 once more. Now dec. 1 st. at neck edge on every row until 29 (34) sts. rem. When length from beg. of armhole shaping matches that of Back, cast off.
Return to rem. 73 (78) sts. Lift the loop (as before) before the first st., and p. to make another st. – 74 (79) sts.
Working first st. as p., work in patt. until 10 patts. have been completed from beg. and rows 1 to 8 have been worked once more.
With right side facing, cast off 27 sts., work to end, working 5 decs. over the first cable – 47 (52) sts.
Next row: Patt. to end.
Next row: Cast off 10 sts., work to end, working 5 decs. over cable patt. of row – 32 (37) sts.
Now dec. 1 st. at neck edge on every row until 29 (34) sts. rem. When length from beg. of armhole matches that of Back, cast off.

Sleeves
With 3¼ mm. needles, cast on 58 (66) sts. Work in k. 2, p. 2 rib (beg. alt. rows p. 2) for 16 rows, inc. 1 st. at each end of last rib row – 60 (68) sts.
Inc. row: Work 30 (32) incs. evenly along rib row – 90 (100) sts.
Change to 4 mm. needles and work in 12 row patt. as for Back until work measures 43 cm. from beg.

To shape top Cast off 6 (7) sts. at beg. of next 2 rows and 4 sts. at beg. of foll. 2 rows – 70 (78) sts.
Dec. 1 st. at each end of every alt. row until 40 (44) sts. rem. Cast off 5 (6) sts. at beg. of next 2 rows, then cast off rem. sts.

TO MAKE UP

Join shoulder seams. Set in sleeves. Join sleeve seams and side seams.

To make up neck edge
With a 4 mm. crochet hook, crochet neatly in double chains along entire neck edge. Crochet a loop for button. Sew on button.

Pale pink cotton sweater in cable and lace has a side neck opening with a crochet edge.

89

Street Legal

INSTRUCTIONS

Back
With 3 mm. needles, cast on 110 (118,

Sleeveless, hip-length top with roll collar is worked in stocking stitch and double rib.
Very Easy

---

126) sts. Work in k. 2, p. 2 rib for 6 cm. Change to 3¾ mm. needles and work in st. st. (see page 12) until work measures 48 cm. from beg.

To shape armholes Cast off 8 sts. at beg. of next 2 rows, and 3 sts. at beg. of foll. 2 rows.
Dec. 1 st. at each end of foll. 7 alt. rows – 74 (82, 90) sts. **.
Cont. straight in st. st. until work measures 20 (21, 22) cm. from beg. of armhole shaping.

To shape shoulders Cast off 9 (10, 11) sts. at beg. of next 2 rows, and 10 (12, 14) sts. at beg. of foll. 2 rows. Slip rem. 36 (38, 40) sts. onto a stitch-holder.

Front
Work as for Back to **. Cont. straight in st. st. until work measures 15 (16, 17) cm. from beg. of armhole shaping, ending with a p. row.

To shape neck Next row: K. 25 (28, 31), turn: cont. on these sts. only. Dec. 1

---

st. at beg. of next and foll. 5 alt. rows. Work 4 rows.

To shape shoulders Cast off 9 (10, 11) sts. at armhole edge, then cast off rem. 10 (12, 14) sts. on foll. alt. row. Slip centre 24 (26, 28) sts. onto a stitch-holder. Rejoin yarn to rem. sts. and work to match first side.

Polo collar
Join right shoulder seam. With 3 mm. needles and right side facing, pick up and k. 29 (30, 31) sts. down left front edge, k. 24 (26, 28) sts. from front, pick up and k. 29 (30, 31) sts. up right front neck, then k. across 36 (38, 40) sts. of back neck – 118 (124, 130) sts.
Work in k. 2, p. 2 rib for 11 cm. Cast off ribwise.
Join left shoulder seam on wrong side, collar on right side.

Armbands
With 3 mm. needles and right side facing, pick up and k. 102 (106, 110) sts. along armhole edge. K. 3 rows. Cast off.

TO MAKE UP

Join side seams and armbands.

Gilda

Smoky blue cardigan in simple stocking stitch has elegant beading of leaves and flowers in small glittery stones.

Easy

MATERIALS

9 (10, 10) 50 g. balls Patons Clansman D.K. in dusky blue (shade 2489); a pair each 3¾ mm. (no. 9) and 4 mm. (no. 8) knitting needles; eight buttons; two shoulder pads; bugle beads and flat-backed round and petal-shaped beads.

TENSION

11 stitches and 15 rows to 5 cm. over stocking stitch, using 4 mm. needles.

MEASUREMENTS

To fit bust 32 (34, 36) in., 82 (86, 92) cm.
Length 23½ (24, 24½) in., 60 (61, 62) cm.
Sleeve seam (all sizes) 18 in., 46 cm.

ABBREVIATIONS

k., knit; p., purl; st(s)., stitch(es); alt., alternate; beg., beginning; cont., continue; dec., decrease; foll., following; inc., increase; rem., remain(ing); rep., repeat; st. st., stocking stitch.

INSTRUCTIONS

Back

With 3¾ mm. needles, cast on 92 (102, 112) sts.
Rib row: * K. 1, p. 1; rep. from * to end.
Rep. rib row eleven times.
Change to 4 mm. needles and cont. in st. st. (see page 12) until work measures 40

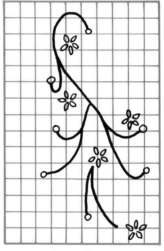

1 sq. = 2 cm.

Diagram shows Right Front.
Reverse diagram for Left Front.

cm. from cast on edge, ending with a p. row.

To shape armhole Cast off 6 sts. at beg. of next 2 rows. Dec. 1 st. at each end of next row and the foll. 3 alt. rows – 72 (82, 92) sts.
Cont. straight until work measures 56 (57, 58) cm. from cast on edge, ending with a p. row.

To shape neck *First side: Row 1:* K. 24 (28, 32) sts., turn. Cont. on these sts.

only, leaving rem. sts. on a spare needle.
Dec. 1 st. at neck edge on the next 10 rows. P. 1 row. Cast off rem. 14 (18, 22) sts.
Second side: Row 1: With right side facing, rejoin yarn to sts. on spare needle, cast off 24 (26, 28) sts., k. to end. Complete to match first side.

Left front

With 3¾ mm. needles, cast on 42 (48, 52) sts. Rib 12 rows as Back.
Change to 4 mm. needles and cont. in st. st. until work measures 40 cm. from cast on edge, ending with a p. row.

To shape armhole Cast off 6 sts. at beg. of next row. P. 1 row. Dec. 1 st. at beg. of next row and the foll. 3 alt. rows – 32 (38, 42) sts. St. st. 10 rows.

To shape neck Cast off 4 sts. at beg. of next row and the foll. 2 alt. rows. K. 1 row. Dec. 1 st. at neck edge on next row and every foll. alt. row until 14 (18, 22) sts. rem. Work straight until Front measures same as Back, ending with a p. row. Cast off.

Right front

Work to match Left Front, reversing shapings.

Sleeves

With 3¾ mm. needles, cast on 52 (54, 56) sts. Rib 12 rows as Back.
Inc. row: Rib 3 (4, 5), * inc. in next st., rib 3; rep. from * to last 5 (6, 7) sts., inc. in next st., rib 4 (5, 6) – 64 (66, 68) sts.
Change to 4 mm. needles and cont. in st. st. until work measures 46 cm. from cast on edge, ending with a p. row.

To shape top Cast off 6 sts. at beg. of next 2 rows. St. st. 2 rows. Dec. 1 st. at each end of next row and every foll.

Gilda

fourth row until 40 sts. rem., then at each end of every alt. row until 18 (20, 22) sts. rem. Work 1 row. Cast off.

Button band

Join shoulders. With 3¾ mm. needles, cast on 13 sts.

Rib row 1: K. 2, * p. 1, k. 1; rep. from * to last st., k. 1.

Rib row 2: K. 1, * p. 1, k. 1; rep. from * to end.

Rep. these 2 rows until band, when slightly stretched, will fit up left front to shoulder, easing around neck shaping. Cast off ribwise. Sew in place. Mark positions for 8 buttons, the first 3 cm. from lower edge, the eighth level with beg. of neck shaping and the rem. 6 spaced evenly between.

Buttonhole band

As Button Band but work until band will fit up right front and across back neck to left shoulder, working butonholes when pin positions are reached thus:

Buttonhole row 1 (right side): Rib 5, cast off 3 sts., rib to end.

Buttonhole row 2: Rib 5, cast on 3 sts., rib to end.

Sew in place, then join cast off edges of bands at left shoulder.

TO MAKE UP

Press as instructed on ball band. Join side and sleeve seams. Set in sleeves. Sew on buttons. Press seams. Use diagram as guide to sew on beads. Sew in shoulder pads.

Country Girls

Simple classics. Knit them either with or without sleeves, with a low V-back and round front neck, or V'd back and front, in cotton or in mohair.

Very Easy

MATERIALS

Long-sleeved V-back sweater 7 (8, 8) 50 g. balls Pingouin Mohair 70 *or* 14 (15, 15) 50 g. balls Pingouin Coton Naturel 8 Fils; a pair each 3¼ mm. (no. 10) and 4 mm. (no. 8) knitting needles.
Sleeveless V-back and -front sweater 8 (9, 9) 50 g. balls Pingouin Coton Naturel 8 Fils *or* 5 (5, 6) 50 g. balls Pingouin Mohair 70; a pair each 3¼ mm. (no. 10) and 4 mm. (no. 8) knitting needles; a circular 3¼ mm. (no. 10) needle for neck.

TENSION

28 stitches and 27 rows to 10 cm. over pattern in both yarns, using 4 mm. needles.

MEASUREMENTS

To fit bust 34 (36, 38) in., 86 (91, 97) cm.
Length 22 (22, 22½) in., 56 (56, 57) cm.
Sleeve seam (all sizes) 17 in., 43 cm.

ABBREVIATIONS

k., knit; p., purl; st(s)., stitch(es); alt., alternate; beg., beginning; cont., continue; dec., decreas(e)(ing); foll., following; inc., increase; m. 1, make 1 stitch by picking up the horizontal loop lying before next st. and working into back of it; patt., pattern; p.s.s.o., pass slip stitch over; rem., remain(ing); rep., repeat; y.r.n., yarn round needle.

INSTRUCTIONS

Long-sleeved V-back sweater

See model (left), facing page

Back
With 3¼ mm. needles, cast on 110 (120, 130) sts. Work in k. 1, p. 1 rib for 6 cm.
Next row: Rib 5 (5, 10), * m. 1, rib 9 (10, 10); rep. from * eleven times, m. 1, rib 6 (5, 10) – 122 (132, 142) sts.
Change to 4 mm. needles and patt. thus:
Row 1: P. 2, * k. 3, p. 2; rep. from * to end.
Row 2: K. 2, * p. 3, k. 2; rep. from * to end.
Row 3: P. 2, * sl. 1, k. 2, p.s.s.o., p. 2; rep. from * to end.
Row 4: K. 2, * p. 1, y.r.n., p. 1, k. 2; rep. from * to end.
These 4 rows form patt. Cont. in patt. until work measures 36 (36, 37) cm. from beg., ending with a row 4 of patt. **

To shape armholes and V-back Cast off 7 sts., patt. 54 (59, 64) sts. including st. on needles after cast off. Leave rem. sts. on a spare needle. Dec. 1 st. at neck edge on next and every foll. third row, *at the same time* cast off 3 sts. at armhole edge on foll. alt. row, then dec. 1 st. at same edge on the foll. 5 alt. rows. Cont. dec. as before at neck edge until 23 (27, 31) sts. rem. When work measures 20 (20, 21) cm. from beg., cast off. Rejoin yarn to rem. sts. and complete other side to match.

Front
Work as for Back to **

To shape armholes Cast off 7 sts. at beg. of next 2 rows and 3 sts. at beg. of foll. 2 rows. Dec. 1 st. at each end of next 5 alt. rows – 92 (102, 112) sts.
Cont. straight until work measures 11 (12, 13) cm. from beg. of armhole shaping.

To shape neck Patt. 30 (35, 40) sts., turn and leave rem. sts. on a spare needle. Dec. 1 st. at neck edge on every row until 23 (27, 31) sts. rem. When armhole measures the same as on Back to shoulder, cast off. Slip centre 32 sts. onto a spare needle. Rejoin yarn to rem. 30 (35, 40) sts. and complete other side of neck to match.

Sleeves

With 3¼ mm. needles, cast on 66 (70, 74) sts. Work in k. 1, p. 1 rib for 6 cm. *Next row:* Rib 3, * m. 1, rib 4; rep. from * fifteen (sixteen, seventeen) times, m. 1, rib 3 – 82 (87, 92) sts.

Change to 4 mm. needles and patt. as for Back, working 1 inc. at each end of every tenth row until there are 92 (97, 102) sts. When work measures 43 cm. from beg., shape armholes by casting off 6 sts. at beg. of next 2 rows and 4 sts. at beg. of foll. 2 rows, then dec. 1 st. at each end of every alt. row until 26 sts. rem. Cast off 4 sts. at beg. of next 2 rows. Cast off rem. 18 sts.

TO MAKE UP

Join right shoulder seam.

Neckband

With 3¼ mm. needles and right side facing, k. up 42 sts. down right back neck, 1 st. from centre, 42 sts. up left back neck, 21 sts. down left front neck, k. across 32 sts. at front, dec. 6 sts. evenly, k. up 21 sts. up right front neck – 153 sts. Work 9 rows in k. 1, p. 1 rib. Cast off ribwise.

Join left shoulder seam and neckband. Set in sleeves. Join side and sleeve seams.

INSTRUCTIONS

Sleeveless top with V-back and front

See model (right), previous page

Back and front

Work as for Back of long-sleeved V-back sweater.

TO MAKE UP

Join shoulder seam.

Neckband

With 3¼ mm. circular needle and right side facing, k. up 42 sts. down right back neck, 1 st. from centre back, 42 sts. up left back neck, 42 sts. down left front neck, 1 st. from centre front and 42 sts. up right front neck. Work 7 rounds in k. 1, p. 1 rib, dec. 1 st. at each side of centre st. at front and back on every alt. row. Cast off ribwise.

Armbands

With 3¼ mm. needles and right side facing, k. up 87 sts. along armhole edge. Work in k. 1, p. 1 rib for 7 rows. Cast off ribwise. Join side and armband seams.